COLLECTING

Baby

Rattles

and *Teethers*

IDENTIFICATION & VALUE GUIDE

Marcia Hersey

Published by

krause publications

700 E. State Street • Iola, WI 54990-0001

Please, call or write us for our free catalog of antiques and collectibles publications.
To place an order or receive our free catalog, call 800-258-0929.
For editorial comment and further information, use our regular business telephone at (715) 445-2214.

Library of Congress Catalog Number: 98-84102
ISBN: 0-87069-766-8
Printed in the United States of America

Dedication

To My Husband

Acknowledgments

With many thanks to Mrs. Jan Laverge, Gabrielle Roth, and Ada Ghiron Segal for their generosity in lending their rattles for this project.

All photographs are by Bernard Palais, New York, except as otherwise noted.

All objects shown are in the collection of the author, except those credited otherwise.

About the Photographer

Mr. Palais is an experienced photographer and educator who has been published in **The New York Times, Newsday, Arts D'Afrique Noire, The Medal,** *and many others. In 1987 he was a recipient of a New York State Council of the Arts grant.*

He has photographed for many well-known institutions, including the Smithsonian Institute, the Fine Arts Museum of Long Island, and the Vanderbuilt Museum.

Mr. Palais is currently a member of the Professional Photographers of America, Photographic Administrators, Inc., Nikon Professional Services, and the Kodak Professional Network. He is a faculty member of International Center of Photography in New York City.

I have often been asked how I got started collecting baby rattles and teethers. Of course, it was by accident!

In the early 1970s, wearing a pendant or similar object on a long chain became popular with women. An acquaintance of mine was wearing an interesting piece one day, and I asked her what it was. The object was a silver and mother-of-pearl baby rattle in the form of a small jester. She said it was an antique she had bought at one of the British ports while on a cruise in the Caribbean.

Shortly after that, my husband and I went on a business trip to Spain. Having time on my hands, I ventured into an antique shop near our hotel. And there—lo and behold—was a whole display of antique baby rattles! They were made of silver and most of them were Spanish, but there were also a few British and American pieces.

Well, the dollar was high then, and I indulged myself buy buying two of them: a clown and a sea monster. The total prices came to less than $100, and I thought I was in collector's heaven! From then on, I kept looking for baby rattles. Having another collector in the family—my husband collects primitive art—I had some guidance to follow although I had not collected anything before.

At about that time, an international directory of collectors was being published. I got myself listed in it and awaited results. Responses were few and far between. Dealers occasionally offered pieces that were too expensive for me to consider purchasing, but how I wish now I had done so—today these pieces are rarely offered on the market, and in retrospect, the prices were reasonable even then!

Then I received a letter from a collector, Ides Cammaert, in Brussels. He, in turn, introduced me to another rattle collector, Heinz Kejyser, from Amsterdam. The three of us developed an enduring personal friendship which lasted until they both passed away. It is from them that I acquired a great deal of the information I have learned about rattles. I owe this book to the memory of these two men who were so giving of their time and knowledge.

After a few years, I had become addicted to collecting. I broadened the range of my collection to include more than just antique baby rattles, but I made all of the usual mistakes a new collector makes: I bought incomplete or damaged rattles; I allowed myself to be swayed by collector's greed; and I was foolishly generous with rattle gifts to friends, not realizing that these examples would never come my way again! But, before I knew it, I had become a serious collector with disciples of my own!

Marcia Hersey
New York, July 1997

P.S.: The first rattle I saw—the one my friend was wearing in 1971—as well as the first rattles I bought in Spain, I later found out, were all reproductions!

Table of Contents

"With what a look of proud command
Thou shak'st in thy little hand
The coral rattle with its silver bells
Making a merry tune"

- "To a Child"

Henry Wadsworth Longfellow

What is interesting about such commonplace toys as rattles and teethers? Why should an entire book be dedicated to them?

The answer is simple. Learning about the history and evolution of baby rattles and teethers down through the ages is to examine almost the entire history of civilization from a single point of view—child-rearing. Every culture has its own theories about the proper way to rear children, and many societies have utilized some very peculiar practices in doing so. Some of these sound very bizarre to us now. Take, for example, the Maya Indians of Pre-Columbian Mexico who used flat boards to compress the infant's head into a long elliptical shape, which they considered beautiful. Examples of this can be seen in the murals they left behind in their temples and in their clay sculptures. The Mayans also dangled a bead in front of their babies' eyes to make them cross-eyed (this was thought to improve the baby's looks).

Although standards of child-rearing have changed, some practices seem to have come full circle in our day. The Western world was shocked in the 1930s when Pearl Buck's heroine in *Oil for the Lamps of China* had her baby and immediately went back to work in the fields. Today, in America, new mothers must fight to stay in the hospital more than twenty-four hours after giving birth. And midwifery, long thought to be unhygienic and dangerous in our germ-conscious modern world, has once again become a widespread and respected profession. Although the famous Dr. Spock approved baby rattles and teethers, there are some pediatricians today who counsel that rattles and teethers can be detrimental to a child's dental development.

To point out a cultural chasm that still exists in baby care, here is a recent American news story: A young mother had her baby taken away by a child welfare service because she had fed the baby taro root when it was four months old. While the current accepted practice in the United States is to withhold solid foods until the baby is nine months old, in the Virgin Islands, the mother's home, babies are given solid food from the very beginning! We can only hope the story had a happy ending!

But what has all this to do with baby rattles and teethers? Baby rattles, too, have remained witnesses to their times. Just as anthropologists can extrapolate from shards and bits of bone or clay to determine the daily life and diet of ancient peoples, baby rattles from around the world can tell us a lot about how people lived and cared for their children.

Baby rattles are naturally connected with the traditional roles of women. In societies where women did the heavy work in the field, or in those cultures where women were mainly concerned with food preparation, bells or other tiny noise-makers were often attached to household tools. In Nepal, the handle of a yogurt churner was hollowed out and small pebbles were placed inside; the rhythmic sound produced kept the baby bundled on her back amused and quiet while she did her work. In India, bells were sometimes attached to the mother's ring or hairpin, which jingled as she cared for the baby. An unusual example of this sort of double-duty object is a little brass foot-scraper with pebbles inside. In a land where children went barefoot, calluses formed, and you can bet children hated having their feet scraped.

They surely needed some diversion during the process! European versions of the double-duty rattle were pap spoons and feeding spoons with bells fastened to them.

In physiological terms, rattles and teethers stimulated most of the child's senses. The color and shininess of the rattles for sight, the bells or pebbles for sound, and how it felt in the hand or mouth for touch. Although not all rattles and teethers have all these attributes, they have at least one or two.

Rattles and teethers generally have as many as four different functions. The first is to amuse the baby and distract it from tears and tempers; the second is to ease the pain of teething; and the third is to ward off evil and protect the child from harm and disease (in which it acts like an amulet or charm). In addition, a fourth function has developed which in some cases has even outweighed the other three. Elaborate and expensive rattles made of precious materials also serve as status symbols, reflecting the wealth and power of the baby's family or of the gift-giver. The importance of each of these functions varies with the individual culture.

According to the *Encyclopedia of World Art* rattles are small hard objects such as seeds, shells, or animal teeth strung together or enclosed in a hard container to produce a clatter when shaken. This definition of a rattle has been broadened in this book to include clappers, where the strikers are attached to the outside of the object, and teethers which are designed to soothe the infant's gums and aid in the weaning process.

No one can know when the first parent discovered that a dried gourd with the seeds inside, would, when shaken, quiet a fretful child, or that a smooth, cool, peeled stick would soothe the baby's gums when it was teething. And, with high infant mortality prevalent throughout the world until almost the present day, it was a logical step to add the protective powers of amulets, charms, and magical materials to the baby's rattle. Even today, rattles are given as traditional christening and baby gifts and carry with them the implied wishes for good health and good fortune.

Collecting baby rattles can be a richly rewarding experience. In addition to the fascination that the playthings of the past hold, the collector will find that many of the rattles are works of art in themselves. The world's most accomplished and skillful gold- and silversmiths have made baby rattles and teethers, and many of the world's most famous painters have done portraits of children holding rattles. Another aspect of rattles to delight the collector is the craftsmanship and ingenuity loving fathers and mothers have put into folk art and home-made rattles.

Then there is also the thrill of the hunt! Searching for rattles is fun. Unfamiliar places often hold unexpected treasures. Looking for rattles while traveling gives a new focus to a trip. The pleasures of research in museums and libraries is another plus for baby rattle collectors. Dating and identifying rattles in pictures and books is an essential task for both the novice and the experienced collector, and museum and library staffs are usually very interested and anxious to help.

This book is intended to furnish ample background information for the collector of baby rattles and teethers. It explores the past and present history of baby rattles, and follows the fads and fashions, traditions, and superstitions that have been related to rattles. Hopefully, the book will inspire new collectors, and encourage collectors of toys, dolls, and silver to expand their interests to a new field. Perhaps it will even spur the casual reader into taking a look at rattles in a new light.

For literally thousands of years, rattles and teethers have been produced in every culture. The simple idea of creating a useful and pleasant toy for babies has been interpreted in a thousand ways. From home-made objects of cloth, wood, straw, or clay to exquisitely worked gold and silver, rattles have always amused, comforted and protected children.

Shiny, bright-colored, smooth or soft, their joyful tintinnabulation echoes through history.

A Brief History of Baby Rattles and Teethers

Rattles and drums were among the first musical instruments used by humans. Probably, after it had been observed that noise could frighten away wild animals, and, by extension, evil spirits, rattles and noisemakers were quickly incorporated into tribal rites and ceremonies. They were used to mark the rhythm of dancers and to invoke the blessings of the gods on crops and fertility and to avert demons.

The earliest rattles were fashioned of bones, animal teeth, shells, and gourds, and they often were decorated with beads, feathers, and incised or painted designs. Because of their ceremonial use, rattles soon became part of a society's sacred objects, usually reserved for the Shaman or medicine man of the tribe.

Although the nature of the very first baby rattle is lost in the mists of time, a baby's response to the sound and movement of a rattle would surely have been noted. From this, the use of rattles to comfort and protect babies would have evolved.

Primitive baby rattles were undoubtedly made from the materials at hand—dried gourds with the seeds inside, or shells strung together on rawhide thongs. The nails and teeth of animals were also used, lending the sympathetic magic of the beast's strength to the infant.

Baby rattles have been found among the relics of many very ancient cultures. The University of Pennsylvania owns a terra-cotta rattle from Tepe Gowra, Mesopotamia, in the shape of a gourd, dating from about 4000 B.C. The Horniman Museum in London has in its collection a small clay rattle in the form of a gourd which is dated about 1350 B.C. (Fig. 1). The earliest Egyptian tombs have yielded little pottery cow rattles, some of which have been dated to the third millennium B.C.

According to Nathaniel Spear, Jr., in his book *A Treasury of Archaeological Bells*, delicate metal work in the form of closed bells was excavated from Luristan gravesites that date from the ninth to the fourth century B.C. His theory is that these bells may have been hung over babies' cradles.

A recent exhibition at the Metropolitan Museum of Art in New York featured pairs of hollow gold spools enclosing seeds or pebbles. These are Grecian artifacts from sixth century B.C. burials. Although their function is not known, they were labeled as rattles, and it is entirely possible that they were used for babies, because they are bright, tinkling, and safe.

Little rattles of baked clay in the shape of dwarfs, hunchbacks, and animals have been found in gravesites at Chandraketugarh in Bengal, India, dating to the second century B.C. In early cultures it was believed that people with unusual physical characteristics also had magical powers, whether for good or evil. The depiction of dwarfs and hunchbacks is a constant thread running through most of the world's folklore (Fig. 2).

HERE IS A BABY'S EARTHENWARE RATTLE. IT HAS PEBBLES INSIDE TO MAKE IT JINGLE. WHEN KING DAVID WAS A BABY HE MAY HAVE PLAYED WITH A RATTLE LIKE THIS ONE.

1360 B.C.

Fig. 1
Illustration, England, early twentieth century. This charming sketch came from a children's Bible storybook. The rattle is possibly based on the clay example from the Horniman Museum in London. Gift of H. Kejyser to the author.

The ancient Greeks used rattles as offerings to the gods of the underworld for the protection of a deceased child. Children holding what appear to be rattles are occasionally depicted on Greek vases, as well.

Later Egyptian tombs, those of the second and first centuries B.C., held animal rattles of clay very similar to those found in India. The Cairo Museum has examples in gold, silver, and bronze in addition to the clay. Some of these bear the cartouche or seal of the family of the dead child (Fig. 3).

Rattle-like objects of quite complicated metal construction were discovered at Herculaneum in Pompeii at excavations undertaken at the end of the eighteenth century (Fig. 4). Rattles in the shape of phalluses were also found, and copies of these were made in France at that time. Children in Cyprus in the Roman period played with small

Fig. 2
Archaic rattle, Chandraketugarh, India, second to first century B.C. Terra-cotta with traces of kaolin, depicting a seated dwarf. Height 5-1/2 inches.

Fig. 3
Rattle, Egypt, second century B.C. Unpainted clay with cat head motif. Length: 4-1/2 inches. From the collection of Ides Cammaert.

clay pig rattles. The pig then was a common sacrifice for the preservation of children.

In the Americas, the Indians of many Pre-Columbian civilizations made rattles for children in painted or incised clay (Fig. 5). Furthermore, rattles and bells have been used since the earliest times in primitive religious and Shamanic ceremonies among the Indians in North America. For instance, rattles were an integral part of solemn or joyful celebrations. They marked the beat of the dancers and were thought to have magical powers in rain-making rites, as well as puberty, marriage, and funeral ceremonies. The combination of dance, prayer, and sound was meant to invoke the goodwill of the gods and to insure good fortune and fertile crops. Similar practices were common in many other tribal societies.

Very little has come down to us about the lives of children during the Middle Ages. Some very early straw and willow rattles have survived from ancient Ireland in that period (Fig. 6). In a few illuminated manuscripts, children can be seen playing simple games, but babies are not often pictured. Other paintings of the late Middle Ages show a rattle with silver bells, scrolled buttress supports, and a crystal handle. Variations of this basic form remained popular for several centuries.

During the medieval period, rattles were used to call the faithful to church services, because the tolling of church bells was reserved for the aristoc-

Fig. 5
Pre-Columbian rattle, Jaina area, Mexico, Late Classic Maya, c. twelfth century A.D. Unpainted clay figure of a deity with a mask on its headdress. Height 3-1/2 inches.

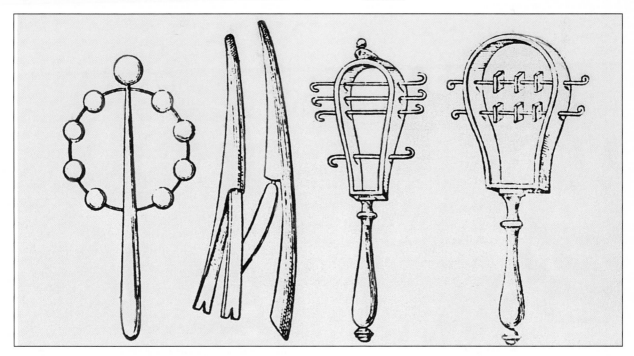

Fig. 4
Clappers and rattles, Pompeii, c. first century B.C. These metal toys were found in eighteenth century excavations.

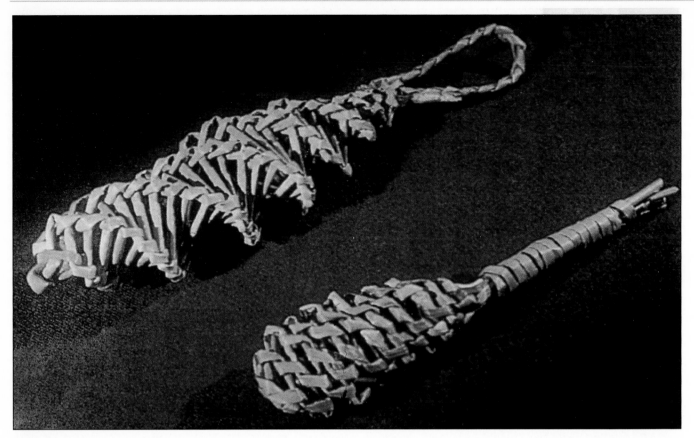

Fig. 6
Two woven rush rattles, Tuam, County Galway, Ireland. Middle Ages. Length: 7 inches (left); 6-1/2 inches (right).

Fig. 7
Coral-and-bells rattle, England, George I, c.1719. Silver with whistle tip, original bells, and coral handle. Hallmark "D." Length 5-1/2 inches.

Fig. 9
Coral-and-bells rattle, England, Regency period, c.1830. Silver with whistle tip, original bells, and short coral handle (may have been ground down). No maker's mark. Length: 4 inches.

Fig. 10
Art Nouveau rattle, U.S., c.1900–1910. Floral design in low relief. Heavy silver with table silver handle, original bells, and whistle tip. Other examples of the same object exist with thick mother-of-pearl handles, so the silver one may have been a replacement. No maker's mark. Length: 5-1/2 inches.

racy. The Victoria and Albert Museum in London has a painted clay rattle in the form of a knight's head. It is probably French, brought to England after the Norman Conquest of Britain in 1066 A.D.

In the early Renaissance, religious paintings often show gold rattles with coral handles held by the Christ Child or offered by the Virgin Mary from a gold chain worn around the neck. Church altar panels and wall paintings, as well as the emerging secular paintings for the aristocracy, continued to depict the Madonna wearing a coral necklace and the Christ Child holding a coral-and-bells rattle until well into the eighteenth century.

The sixteenth century saw the fuller development of the coral-and-bells type of baby rattle. Its roots lay in the earlier Spanish and Italian prototypes. The coral-and-bells form consisted of an elongated or bulbous stem with small bells attached and with a coral teething stick at one end. Whistle tips were a later addition. In its many variations, the coral-and-bells remained the classic style until the middle of the nineteenth century. (Fig. 7)

In eighteenth century Europe the popularity of baby rattles and teethers and their widespread use among the children of the noble class is confirmed by the number of references to baby rattles in European literature. Jean-Jacques Rousseau (1712-1798) in his famous treatise on child-rearing and education, *Emile* (1762), denounces the elaborate rattles of his time and suggests toys made of natural materials instead. Thomas Carlyle and Francis Quarles also mention baby rattles in their works, and Lewis Carroll even wrote a couplet about them!

The custom of giving elaborate rattles to royal babies has persisted into modern times. In Egypt, King Faud I, born in 1868, was given a rattle with a jade handle, topped with a replica of a crown decorated with emeralds and diamonds. This is now in the Koubbeh Palace collection in Cairo. And at the birth of Princess Juliana of Belgium in 1909, the royal family was presented with a silver-gilt rattle with diamonds and emeralds and carved with the symbols of the nine provinces of the country.

Most of what can be learned about European antique baby rattles and teethers must be gleaned from paintings. It is quite a rich harvest! Portraits of royal children are plentiful and many of them show the children with rattles. Most of the rattles were of gold or silver and were considered family treasures to be handed down from generation to generation. A family in Brussels today is able to

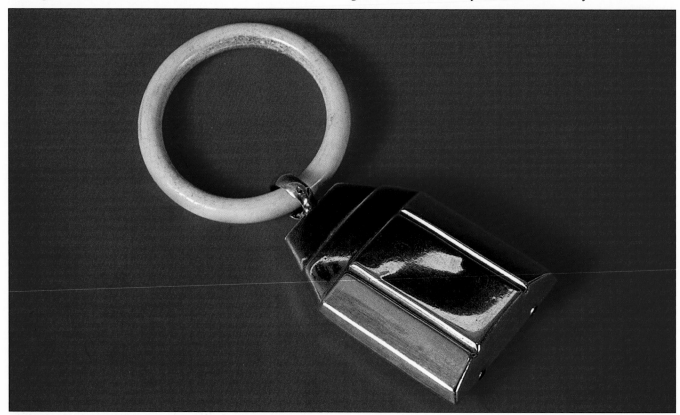

Fig. 11
Art Deco rattle, France, c.1925. Silver in geometric design with ivory handle. French hallmark on loop. Height: 1-3/4 inches.

trace its rattle back twelve generations!

One of the earliest portraits of a royal child with a rattle is that of Edward VI, son of Henry VIII of England. The picture shows a two- or three-year-old boy, richly dressed, carrying a gold rattle of pierced and embossed design (Fig. 8). The painting is accredited to "circle of Holbein" and dates to the mid-sixteenth century. It is one of several versions of this subject, and was formerly in the collection of the National Museum in Washington, D.C.

Paintings by Rembrandt, Velasquez, and Van Dyke, among others, illustrate that rattles were in common use in Holland, Spain, and England throughout the seventeenth and eighteenth centuries. The decorative style of this period was inclined to be heavy and ornate and these elements were carried over into the baby rattles of those times as well.

In the New World, colonists in America followed the European styles closely. The Puritans believed that children were just small adults and capable of sin! Their philosophy was opposed to pleasure and luxury of any sort; work and prayer sufficed. Later colonists, including the Dutch settlement in New York, were more liberal in their views of child-rearing, and rattles and other toys were in general use.

By the time of the American Revolution, expert silversmiths were already working in New York, Boston, Philadelphia, and Baltimore, but rattles from the mother country held snob appeal. This was also true of the Spanish colonists in Latin and South America, who valued objects made in Spain.

In Europe, following the baroque and rococo tastes of the previous two centuries, the more restrained Georgian and Regency styles evolved, dating roughly between the ascension to the throne of England by George I in 1711 to the beginning of the Victorian era in 1832. Elegant simplicity and exquisite proportions characterized the designs of this period in architecture and furniture, and this neo-classic influence can be seen in the baby rattles of the time as well (Fig. 9).

In contrast to these somewhat austere lines in Georgian, Regency, and early Victorian styles, later Victorian decoration tended to be complicated and fussy. In architecture, interior design, and clothing, the "Gilded Age" was synonymous with excessive details. Baby rattles and teethers reflected this taste, but changes were on the way.

Although molded and pressed metals appeared as early as 1800, most silverwork was hand-crafted. By the 1870s, though, the day of the individual

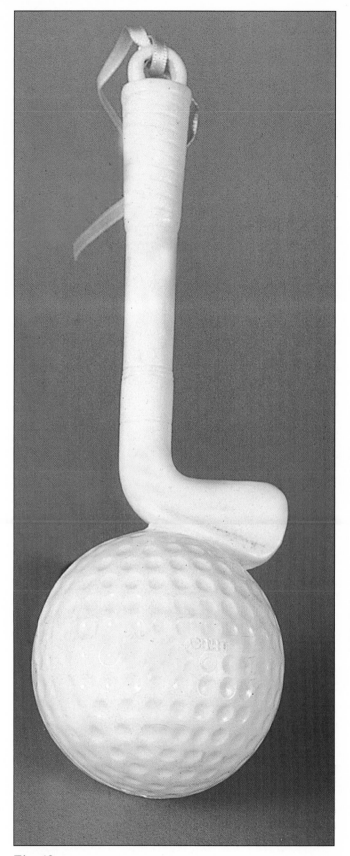

Fig. 12
Golf rattle, U.S. c. 1935–1940. Molded white plastic rattle of club and golf ball, with loop on top for ribbon or ring. Original Binkytoy label. Height: 6-1/2 inches.

Fig. 13
Adult pacifier, U.S., 1982. The ultimate luxury object—gold and diamonds with a crystal stub handle.
Length: 2 inches. Courtesy Sidney Mobell.

silver or goldsmith was drawing to a close. They were replaced by manufacturers who were able to turn out larger numbers of items at less cost. The public demand for luxury goods had expanded enormously with the rise of the middle class and the widespread effects of the industrial revolution. Machine-stamped rattles were produced in abundance, using sentimental themes of cherubs, flowers, and hearts. By the end of the Victorian era, ivory and mother-of-pearl handles were replacing the traditional coral.

At the turn of the twentieth century, artists started to reject the elaborations of the previous generations. A new art movement arose, known as Art Nouveau. Led by William Morris in England and followed by other artists on the continent, Art Nouveau based its philosophy on a return to the simplest forms in nature. Curved lines and stylized floral patterns expressed these ideas, especially in the decorative arts. Art Nouveau had a strong influence in France and Belgium, and held sway until the first World War in the graphic arts and interior decoration. The baby rattles of the era reflect this (Fig. 10).

Following the war, tastes and attitudes changed quickly. Worldwide upheaval and new technolo-gies led to new visions in art and society. Again, a different approach developed in the arts. The style, known as Art Deco or Art Moderne, was adopted by creative artists throughout Europe. France, forever in the vanguard of new ideas, produced the first "Art Moderne" exhibition in Paris in 1925, which helped to spread the style throughout the art world. In France Jacques Ruhlmann and Ellen Grey made furniture and Coco Chanel replaced the corsets of the past with new freedom in costume. In Germany, Jugendstil revolutionized the graphic arts, and the Vienna Secession produced household objects and home furnishings with the clean new lines and bright colors.

Art Deco, with its geometric lines, minimal decoration, and restraint of detail, was not universally accepted, but its influence can be traced in modern design until the present day. Baby rattles in the Art Deco style were made in the 1920s and '30s; the ones which have survived have a nostalgic charm, but the general public seemed to prefer more conventional motifs (Fig. 11).

New technologies developed during World War II produced synthetic materials not seen before. Molded plastics were used for furniture and household items. Nylon replaced silk for hosiery.

And other new textiles for clothing and home furnishings flooded the marketplace.

Baby rattles, too, were soon made of plastics, and rattles and toys made of celluloid and Bakelite were readily available. Traditional silver or silver-plated rattles, however, continued to be the accepted expensive baby gift at birth or christening.

As the middle class grew prosperous and more leisure time became available, new hobbies and interests came into the lives of people in the industrialized nations. The emerging enthusiasm for sports in the late nineteenth and early twentieth century produced rattles that echoed these pastimes. Football, golf, and tennis themes in baby rattles soon appeared in the market (Fig. 12; see also Fig. 107). Also, new developments in technology were translated into rattles which depicted airplanes, radios, and telephones.

Silver manufacturers continued to make rattles with handles identical to those of their table silver, and famous jewelry firms like Cartier and Tiffany in New York also began to make beautiful silver and gold rattles. The classic dumbbell shape is still the top seller. Occasionally, these firms offer a modified version of an antique rattle.

The broad variety of plastics now being made offers an overwhelming choice in baby rattles. Hard and soft vinyls and polyurethane objects are easy to clean and very inexpensive. If the baby beats its plastic rattle on its highchair too often, it is no problem to replace the rattle with another.

Forward-looking manufacturers today work with educators to develop safe and attractive mass-produced toys, including rattles and teethers, that will help foster the child's development. Hand-crafted rattles are still being made, chiefly in wood, by individual carvers in the back-to-the-natural movement of our times.

And, in the personally stressful atmosphere of urban life today, adults can feel the need of a pacifier or rattle, too. These luxury objects are designed to relieve stress and anxiety and aid meditation, control bad habits like smoking, and serve almost the same functions they do for babies (Fig. 13 and 14).

Baby rattles, although not leaders in design, have always very quickly followed the newest styles. Just as costume, furniture, and interior decoration give an insight into the way people lived, baby rattles, too, give us a picture of their times.

Fig. 14
Adult rattle, U.S. 1996. Painted wood and papier mâché, designed as a New Age meditation aid. Made by California artist Charlie Tweddle. Length 10-1/2 inches.

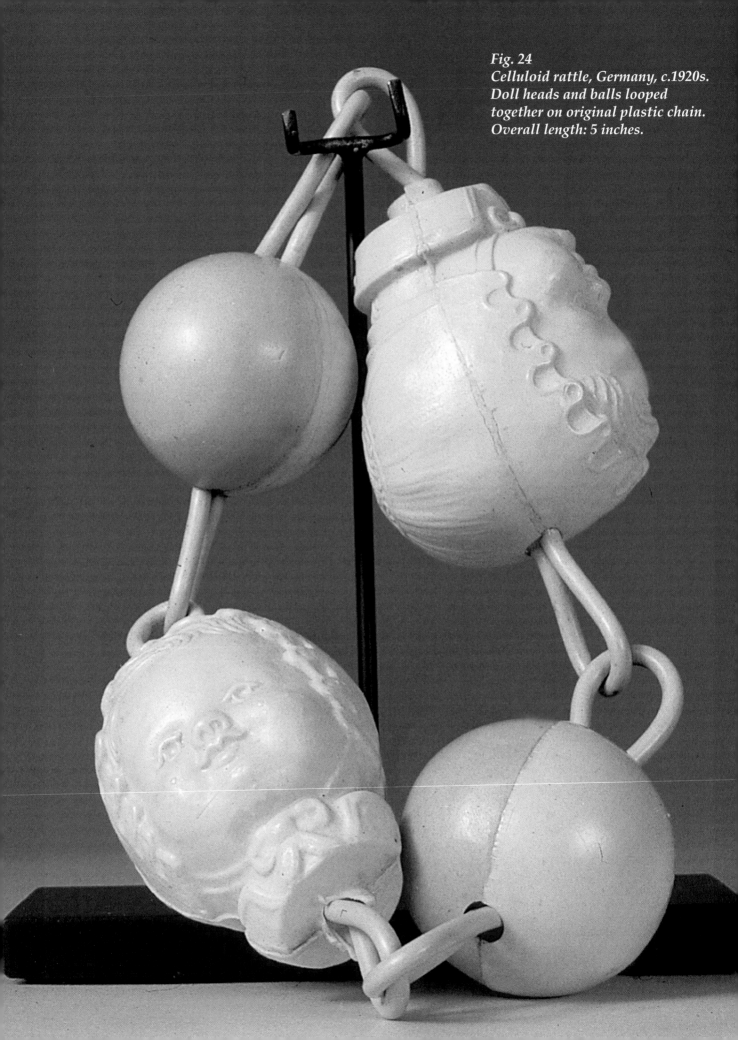

Fig. 24
*Celluloid rattle, Germany, c.1920s.
Doll heads and balls looped
together on original plastic chain.
Overall length: 5 inches.*

Baby Rattle and Teether Forms: Jingles, Tinkles, and Clatters

How remarkable it is that there is an amazing similarity among the forms of rattles from all times and from all over the world. Although design and decoration of baby rattles have followed closely the tastes of each culture and country, there has always been surprising consistency in form.

There are four basic shapes which rattles take, plus a few others which developed at a later date but are still widely used. The first kind is a closed container containing pebbles or seeds which knock against the inner surface of the container when shaken. The second major category of form is the clapper where external bells or beads are attached to a central drum or post. Shells, discs, balls, or similar objects strung together on a cord or stitched to a chain constitute the third type of rattle. Finally, there is the sistrum, where beads or balls are strung on a rod and surrounded by a rigid frame. The number of variations on these simple forms is limited only by the imagination and ingenuity of the maker.

The earliest baby rattles of the enclosed form were probably dried gourds with the seeds inside (Fig. 15). This was followed later by little animals or figures of clay with pebbles or seeds inside which rattled when shaken. More modern versions include the drum (Fig. 16) and the mallet (Fig. 17). Usually, these rattles have a stick or handle of some sort. The dumbbell shape is another modification of the enclosed type of rattle. This is simply a rod with a ball at either end. The pebbles, or whatever noisemaker is used, are generally in the end balls, or in the rod, if it is hollow (Fig. 18). Dumbbell rattles, still popular today, are most often made of silver and frequently have shaped rods which make it easier for a child to grasp. Latter-day rattles in the form of figurines, dolls, animals, and balls are all examples of the closed container style.

Another early and widespread enclosed form of rattle is the one made of twisted basketry (Fig. 19). This is commonly a spiral woven ball of straw, willow, reed, or raffia, with a handle of the same material, and seeds within. These rattles have been found in times and places as disparate as medieval Ireland, eighteenth century France, nineteenth century America and modern Mexico, Russia, and Africa.

Primitive Amazon tribes of Brazil and Equador used similar rattles when the first European explorers arrived. Perhaps the popularity of woven rattles is explained by the easy availability of the material and the comparative ease of manufacture by the basket-maker. To the novice, however, such rattles look quite sophisticated and difficult to make.

The clapper is still another form of baby rattle that has existed for several centuries. In its earliest appearance in ancient China, it was made as a little drum with two external beads or stones attached to act as strikers. This is the traditional type of baby rattle still found throughout the Far East and Southeast Asia. Leather, paper, wood, or silver were used to form the drum, and the handle was usually of wood. Creative toy makers throughout the world have adapted the clapper style. It can be as plain as a cluster of

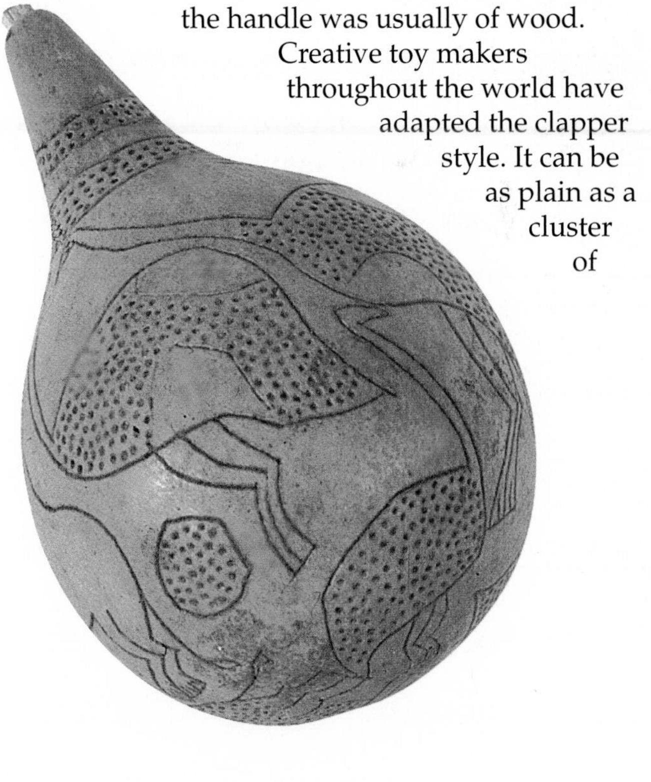

Fig. 15
Gourd rattle, Kenya, c.1970. Incised with traditional bird and animal patterns. Length: 4-1/2 inches.

Fig. 16
Drum rattle, Cherokee Nation, U.S., 1990. Small toy drum with feather trim and tribal symbols on painted leather with a wooden handle. Length: 14 inches.

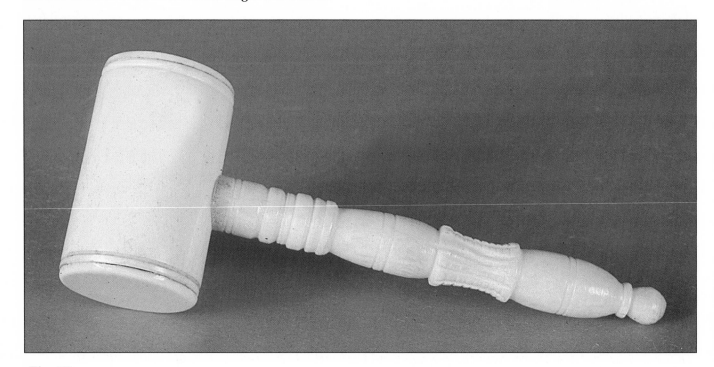

Fig. 17
Scrimshaw rattle, New England, U.S., c.1840. Whalebone rattle in mallet shape. Length: 5 inches.

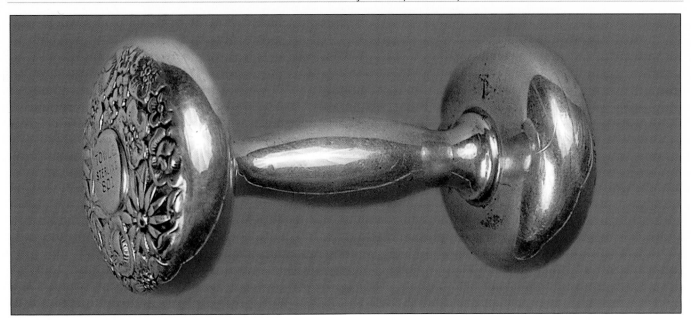

Fig. 18
Dumbbell rattle, U.S., c.1910. Heavy silver with embossed floral design at ends. Marked "Sterling" and stamped with the maker's name, Towle. Length: 3 inches.

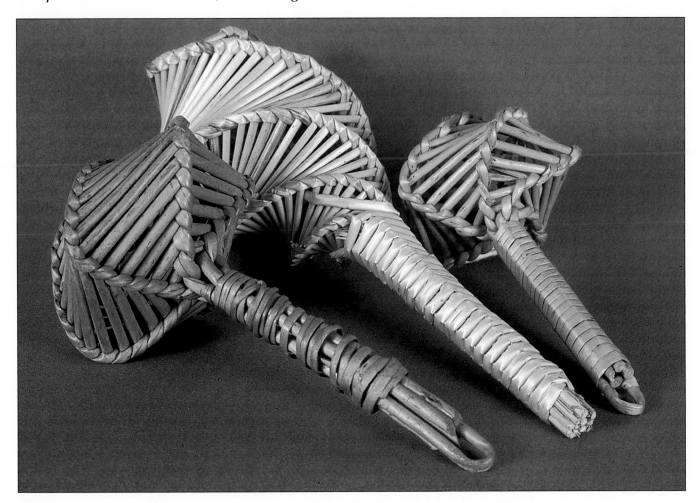

Fig. 19
Twisted straw rattles. Three examples from around the world. Left: France, copy of eighteenth century rattle; center: U.S., early twentieth century; right: India, late twentieth century. Lengths: 6 to 7 inches each.

bells on a simple wooden stick or as elaborate as chased silver with a coral handle (Fig. 20 and 21). This style was also the one mainly used for figurative motifs from the late nineteenth century on, usually with a silver figure, bells, and a mother-of-pearl handle.

The first coral-and-bells rattles were made in a simple clapper shape, but soon developed into the more complicated buttress and baluster styles. The baluster is an elongated or rounded bulb shape and takes its name from the flower bud of the pomegranate. The pomegranate has been associated with fertility since Biblical times, and this may account for the use of this form in baby rattles. The baluster may have two or even three tiers of balls, usually open, and a handle of coral, crystal, or agate.

The coral-and-bells rattle dates back to at least the fifteenth century, as can be seen in the portraits of royal children and the religious paintings of the time. With some modifications, the style remained the classic type of status rattle until the mid-nineteenth century. Embossing, pierced-work, and delicate engraving called "brightwork" were lavished on these rattles by the leading goldsmiths and silversmiths of each era.

Teethers and teething sticks of similar design, without bells, were also made by these craftsmen. People may have felt that the teethers were safer for the babies than the rattles with their delicate, swallowable bells, and quite possibly, teethers were a bit less expensive. Today, antique rattles and teethers of the same age and quality cost about the same price.

It has been suggested that the coral-and-bells design was originally based on the silver or gold finials which are inserted at the top of the handles

Fig. 20
Folk Art rattle, U.S., 1980s; wooden stick with metal bells, reproduction of mid-nineteenth century style. Length: 5 inches.

Fig. 21
Coral-and-bells rattle, England, c.1740. Silver teether shape with two bells, whistle tip, and coral handle. Initialed "E.M." No maker's mark. Length: 5 inches.

Fig. 22
Jester rattle, England, 1909. Stylized jester figure in silver, with whistle tip, two bells, and stub mother-of-pearl handle. Birmingham mark. Length: 3-1/2 inches.

Fig. 23
Teething-ring rattles, U.S., early twentieth century. Left: Ivory ring with embossed silver bell, diameter: 2-1/2 inches; right: silver ring with shell-shaped bells, marked "Sterling." Diameter: 1-7/8 inches.

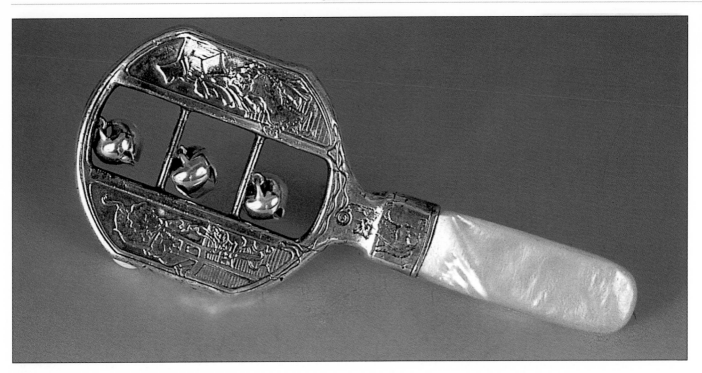

Fig. 25
Sistrum-type rattle, U.S., 1910. Silver rattle with modified stub mother-of-pearl handle. Frame is embossed on all sides with storks and other animals. Length: 4-1/2 inches.

Fig. 26
Spinner rattle, U.S., c.1940s. Plastic mermaid holding clear plastic ball with tiny sea creatures inside which rattle when spun. Probably designed as a bath toy. Original box, showing price of 39¢. Length: 7 inches.

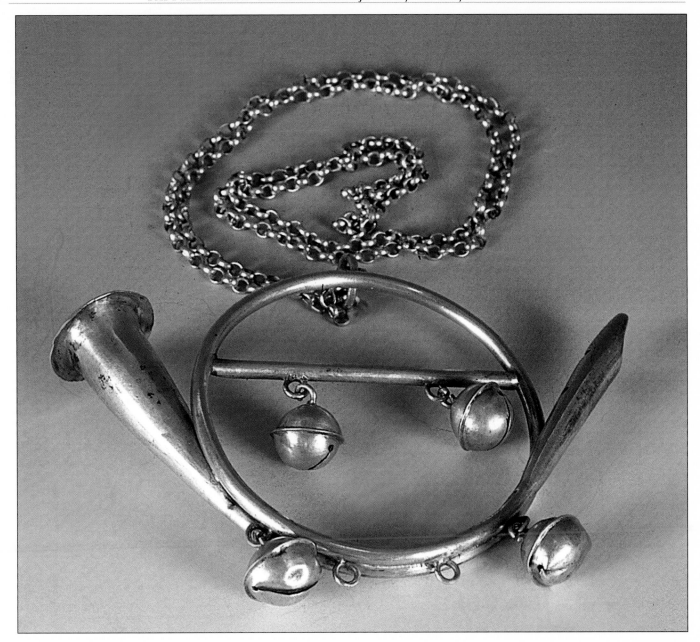

Fig. 27
French horn rattle, France, 1920s or '30s. Silver with whistle tip. Two bells are missing. A silver chain accompanied rattle. Diameter: 2-1/2 inches.

of the Scroll of the Ark in the Jewish religion. Interestingly enough, legend has it that these decorations, called *rimonim*, were themselves based on the form of the pomegranate.

Another theory has it that the coral-and-bells was adapted from the costume of the court jester, who traditionally wore a cap with bells and carried some sort of rattling object in his hands. The jester has certainly remained a frequently used figure in rattles. From the French Punchinelle of the eighteenth century to the plastic clown rattles of our day, the image of the jester has delighted children throughout the years.

Whistles first appeared in the tips of the coral-and-bells rattles and teethers around 1700, and have continued to be a part of many different types of rattles. Very young children had to depend on the nurse or mother to blow the whistle, of course, but what child wouldn't want to make a noise itself as soon as he or she was able to?

Simpler versions of the coral-and-bells were made into the late Victorian period; the coral stick was gradually replaced by one of ivory or mother-of-pearl.

Around the turn of the twentieth century, the "stub" handle on rattles came into general use. The

Fig. 28
Whimsy rattle, U.S., late nineteenth century. Carved from one piece of wood in openwork design; has wooden ball visible inside. Marked 1887 on handle. Length: 5 inches.

stub is basically a clapper type of rattle with two silver bells. It features a broad, flattened handle of mother-of-pearl surmounted by a silver top in a pressed design (Fig. 22). The motif of the rattle ranged from floral designs, animals, and angels to fairy-tale and Mother Goose characters. Because the stub rattles were mass-produced and far less expensive than craftsman's work, they remained in fashion until World War I. An American mail-order catalogue of 1912 offered several styles of stub rattles priced from $1.25 to $3.75 apiece.

The third general type of rattle is one which utilizes different kinds of objects strung together that make an attractive sound when shaken. Shells, beads, and the teeth, claws, and even toenails of animals—items that were readily available—were the earliest materials used for creating this type of rattle. These items were oftentimes threaded on a cord of woven straw or a rawhide thong. The materials used changed as time went on, and in the Victorian era (Fig. 23) it was not uncommon to have a rattle made of silver, ivory, or mother-of-pearl with little bells attached to it. Celluloid versions were made in the 1920s and '30s (Fig. 24), and Bakelite was used in similar fashion in the 1940s. This form is still in use today, as is evident in the multitude of plastic variations of this style.

The sistrum shape of rattle, known since the days of Pompeii in the first century A.D., is only occasionally used today. The form is reminiscent of a small abacus. Balls or beads are strung on a rod, which is enclosed in a rigid frame. A few interpretations of the sistrum have been made in modern times, but the shape is awkward for a child to handle (Fig. 25).

Other elements in rattle design have evolved as time elapsed. The spinner, which held a ball or pinwheel in a rigid half-circle frame can be seen as an outgrowth of the sistrum style. Some spinner rattles have the pebbles inside the center, and others have external bells. Pierced work and filigree metalwork were often used for these rattles. Plastic rattles can be found today following the same principle (Fig. 26).

The use of a miniature drum-shape for a rattle has been found in many cultures since the earliest times. Reproducing the forms of other musical instruments for baby rattles emerged in the nineteenth century. The most common instances of these have been the trumpet, the bugle, and the French horn (Fig. 27). The mouthpiece is finished with a whistle, and the bells are attached externally. Tambourines also seemed a natural style for a baby rattle, and examples exist in silver from the 1880s. Plastic tambourine rattles are made today in China and Japan.

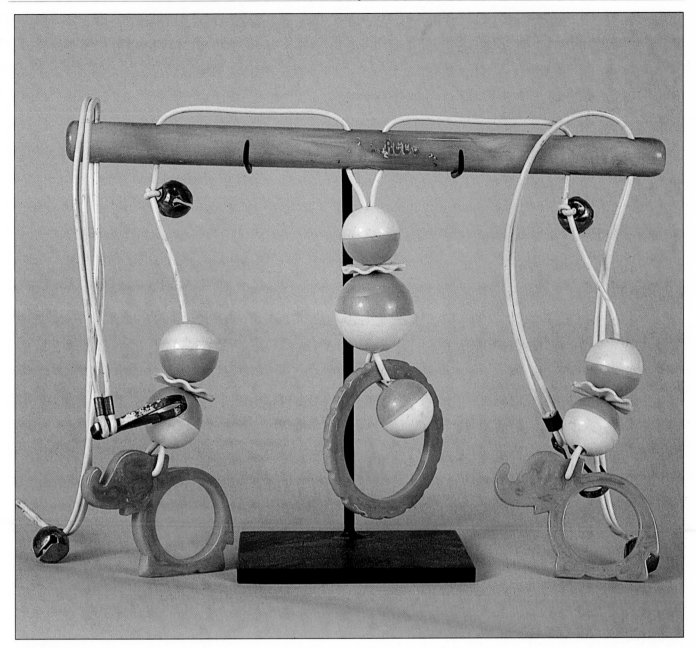

Fig. 29
Crib toy, U.S., 1930s. Metal bells, plastic balls, and Bakelite teething rings suspended on a rod. This was placed across the crib so baby could pull down the teethers and hear the bells tinkle. Width: 11 inches.

Whimsies, whittled of one piece of wood, became a folk-art version of the baby rattle in rural areas in the United States and England in the nineteenth century. Designed to exhibit the skill of the carver, whimsies could have a solid post with rings sliding up and down (sistrum type) or fancy openwork with a ball of wood inside (enclosed type) (Fig. 28). These virtuoso craftsmen also made other objects in the whimsy style, but the baby rattles have the most appeal.

Crib toys which consisted of dangling bells or teething sticks strung over the baby's crib are a relative of baby rattles. They encouraged the infant to reach up and grasp the shiny object of the soothing teething stick. The mobile hanging crib toys of today are descendants of this style (Fig. 29).

Hundreds of variations of the basic rattle forms have been invented. From the crudest constructions in primitive tribes through all the vicissitudes of taste through the ages, the skill and imagination of craftsmen and loving parents has gone into the creation of these universal playthings. One may be sure that, even a thousand years from today, children will be playing with rattles that in some form echo the original rattle shapes.

*Fig. 39
Artisan's rattle, U.S., 1990. Two-tone
natural wood carved in a variation of the
clapper shape. Made by Mossy Creek,
Arkansas, craftsman. Length: 5-1/4
inches.*

Baby Rattle and Teether Materials: What Are They Made Of?

What are rattles made of? The answer to that question is: Almost anything you can think of that can be put together to make a pleasant noise! Rattles have been made of straw, reed, and rattan (Fig. 30). They have been made of wood, ivory, whalebone, and mother-of-pearl. They have been made of animal claws, teeth, and toenails. They have been made of tin, leather, plastic, and paper. And they have also been made of gold and silver, cloth, snuffboxes, gourds, and shells.

In the early days of human history, the natural materials at hand were used in rattles, both for tribal rites and for children. Relics of these have been found in archaeological excavations from ancient cultures around the world. These societies produced rattles in a variety of natural materials and clay. Turtle shells were made into rattles by many North and South American Indian tribes: the rattles were formed by fastening two shells together to make a clatter when shaken. Shells, gourds, and animal teeth were also widely used. To protect the tribe, as well as the child, the rattles often had fetish material added, along with feathers, beads, and painted or incised symbolic decorations.

As civilizations developed, a greater variety of toys came into being. As early as the eleventh century B.C., clay rattles in the form of little animals began to appear. The Horniman Museum in London has an example of one of these dating to 1350 B.C. Many clay rattles dating as far back as the third century B.C. have been found in India, Mesopotamia, and Egypt. Pre-Columbian peoples in the Americas also made clay rattles for children that have been unearthed from early burial sites.

Coral, used for the sticks of rattles and teethers, has a long history. Red coral, or *Corrallum rubrum*, to give it its proper name, is a natural product of the sea. It is formed out of the calcified remains of millions of tiny sea creatures. Although black coral and white coral can be found in tropical waters around the world, the red coral of the Mediterranean was the variety that held associations with health and protection since ancient times.

The belief that coral held magical and healing powers seems to have arisen quite early in recorded history. The early Greeks and Egyptians often wore coral necklaces and amulets (as can be seen in their jewelry and other grave artifacts).

The origins of the superstitions surrounding coral can possibly be traced to the myth of Perseus and the Gorgon, Medusa. According to Ovid's "Metamorphoses," the twigs that lay under Medusa's severed head when it was cast into the sea became red coral and therefore associated with blood. Somehow this story became connected with triumph over disease and evil. Because coral hardens permanently when it is taken out of water, it was also thought that it would help harden children's teeth and gums, while warding off illness and ill fortune.

Whatever its origin, this belief about coral as protector and healer seems to have taken hold of the European imagination for several centuries. Paracelsus, a German physician of the sixteenth century, recommended the use of ground coral for medicinal purposes.

During the Middle Ages and early Renaissance, paintings of the Holy Family in many European cathedrals show both the Madonna and Child wearing coral necklaces. Coral necklaces are also often depicted in ex-voto paintings in churches. These were naïve paintings offered to the saints in gratitude for a prayer that had been answered. A child's recovery from serious illness was often the theme of these pictures.

By the fifteenth century, gold rattles with coral handles began to appear in religious paintings, and variations of the style continued to be seen in portraits of children for several centuries. Even today, in parts of southern Italy and South America, the *figa*, a coral amulet in the shape of a root or a hand, is worn to avert the evil eye and to keep the wearer from harm.

During the next several centuries, the coral-and-bells form of baby rattle was developed, refined, and adapted by skilled gold- and silversmiths throughout Europe and the British Isles. Sometimes the coral handle was replaced by carefully worked crystal or carnelian. In Northern Europe, where coral was extremely difficult to obtain, the tooth of a wolf or a wild boar might be

Fig. 30
Woven straw rattles, 1990s. Left to right: Ecuador, India, Burkina Faso, and Mexico. Heights: 5 to 6-1/2 inches.

substituted for the coral teether. Because these rattles were intended for the aristocracy, each rattle was individually wrought and decorated with pierced-work, engraving, embossing, or repoussé work. Besides gold and silver, vermeil, a gilded silver emulating pure gold, was often used. Two or three tiers of bells, usually open, were added as time went by (Fig. 31).

The newly explored and colonized territories of the world brought ivory to Europe in the eighteenth century. Ivory objects became popular in France and Belgium (with colonies in Africa) and England (with imports from India). These items included carved and polished souvenir elephants,

pipes, and boxes. Baby rattles and handles for rattles and teethers were prominent among them (Fig. 32).

By the early nineteenth century, the developing Industrial Revolution had introduced a wide variety of consumer goods that were pressed or molded by machines. By Victorian times, mass-produced rattles in silver, silver-plate, and tin were quite easily available to the middle classes (Fig. 33).

Ivory and whalebone carvings by Napoleonic prisoners of war and sailors away on long voyages produced delicate objects to be sent home. These included pie-cutters, yarn-holders, cribbage boards, and of course, baby rattles and teethers.

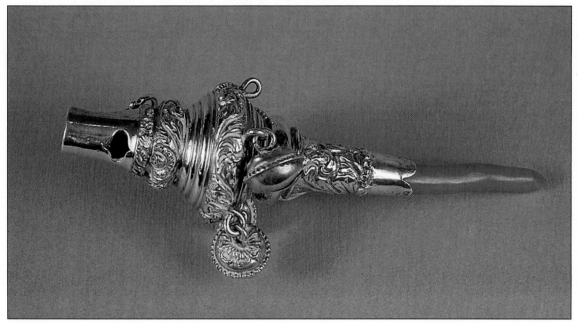

Fig. 31
Coral-and-bells rattle, England, mid-nineteenth century. Silver with silver bells and
coral handle. Length: 4-1/2 inches.

Fig. 32
Ivory rattle, France, early nineteenth century. Pierced and carved ivory. Prisoner's or sailor's work from
the Napoleonic Wars period. Length: 5 inches.

Very early in the eighteenth century, a London watchmaker, Christopher Pinchbeck (1670-1732), concocted an alloy of copper and zinc similar to brass, but with more copper, which was named after him. Its color closely resembled that of gold, and it was soon being used for watches, cheap jewelry, and etuis, little cases that hold manicure utensils or sewing tools. Some baby rattles were made of pinchbeck, as were doll rattles, but gilded silver was more commonly used to imitate gold. While the invention of this alloy was claimed by Pinchbeck and bears his name, similar alloys were used throughout Europe well into the late Victorian era.

Another Englishman, Alexander Parkes, is credited with the invention of celluloid in 1856. It was among the first of the man-made materials to gain wide public acceptance. For a long time, celluloid was made into vanity table pieces like mirror and brush frames, and used for toys and dolls. Celluloid was easily colored and molded and was quite inexpensive, but it was highly inflammable. Toys, dolls, and rattles continued to be made of celluloid up until World War II. These objects are much sought-after today by collectors (Fig. 34).

Fig. 33
Heart-shaped rattles, U.S., late nineteenth century. Machine-made rattles in silver. The rings, which were probably mother-of-pearl, are missing. Left: length 2 inches; center: floral designs in relief, length 2-1/2 inches; right: Height 1-1/4 inches.

Bakelite, a much harder and more durable resin, was developed in the United States in 1909 by L.H. Baekeland, a German chemist. Its versatility and strength soon supplanted the more fragile celluloid in the manufacturing of many household objects. Bakelite had many imitators, including Marblette and Catalin, but Bakelite is now the generic term for all of these similar resins. In the 1930s and '40s these materials were used extensively for jewelry, which is now highly prized by collectors. Some toys and baby rattles were also made of these materials, but Bakelite could not produce the very bright colors found in celluloid

toys, and were less appealing to a child (Fig. 35). Both Bakelite and celluloid held their places of prominence in the marketplace until the new plastics developed after World War II took over.

Despite the increasing use of the new synthetic materials, baby rattles continued to be made of silver, silver plate, tin, and wood. Tin toys, painted or unpainted, were manufactured as early as 1845 and were made until the 1940s when most metals were pre-empted for the war effort. Tin horse-drawn trolley-cars, trains, and (later) airplanes, were toys treasured throughout the western world. The painted tin rattles of the early twentieth century give a delightful glimpse of what childhood was like in those days. Little boys in their sailor suits and little girls in their pinafores are shown playing with hoops, riding on pony carts, see-saws, and swings.

Stamped and unpainted baby rattles in tin were also manufactured in large numbers. The most popular shape was a mallet with a wood or tin handle that had a whistle at the tip (Fig. 36). One advertisement in the 1890s offered a dozen tin rattles for $2.75 wholesale; painted ones were $4.00 the dozen!

It should be mentioned that all the while fond fathers had kept on whittling wood rattles and doting mothers had made cloth doll and animal rattles, but these homemade gifts of love rarely survived depredations of active children and few old examples remain (Fig. 37).

By the 1870s, manufacturing processes had largely taken over the work of the individual craftsman. Factories making table silver soon began to make baby rattles, too. Ivory and mother-of-pearl teething rings and handles replaced coral, which had lost its appeal, perhaps, when the germ theory of disease was finally accepted.

Manufacturers of silver and silver plate often used the same handles on their rattles as they did on their knives and forks. Many companies famous at the time have since disappeared, but Wallace, Weber, Whiting, and the Unger Brothers were among those who made baby rattles. Today baby rattles in sterling silver are still offered by companies like Tiffany and Cartier as lavish baby gifts. Occasionally, these firms will present a modified version of an antique rattle in their Christmas catalogues.

After World War II, a vast array of new materials came into use, many of them derived from war-time innovations. Hard and soft vinyls, polyurethane, and other plastics soon became the medium for many household and decorative articles. Toys, dolls, and baby rattles and teethers were especially adaptable for manufacture in plastics, because they could be made cheaply, could be easily cleaned, and were replaceable at very little cost. Silver and silver-plated rattles continued to be made, but they were, and still are, relatively expensive (Fig. 38).

Progressive toy firms today are working

with educators to design toys which are safe, pleasant to hold, and serve to promote the baby's color and form perception and other learning areas. Many of these toys, including rattles, are made of smoothly polished wood and painted with non-toxic material. In addition, there are still wood carvers working to make individual and distinctive toys, including rattles and teethers as part of a growing trend to return to natural sources and

Fig. 34
Celluloid rattle, U.S., 1920s. Painted celluloid stork holding a baby. Length: 7 inches.

Fig. 36
Tin rattle, U.S., late nineteenth century. Mallet-shaped with simple pressed design. It has a tin handle with a whistle tip. Length: 6-1/2 inches.

Fig. 35
Bakelite rattle, U.S., 1940s. Discs and beads hang through a Bakelite teether on a chain. Length 3-1/2 inches.

hand-made objects. Woven straw rattles are still being made around the world, too (Fig. 39).

Teethers, whose function has been to soothe gums and aid in the weaning of a child, seem to have had a humbler past than rattles. They have been made from a variety of materials, but their development has followed a simple path. In ancient times a peeled willow stick was sufficient to soothe the baby's gums. Since then many different materials have been employed to make teethers, including ivory, bone, and mother-of-pearl. By the beginning of the twentieth century nipple shapes in ivory became quite popular. In modern times pacifiers and teethers with nipples in rubber or plastic are the most common, because they can easily be cleaned and effectively quiet a child. The highly decorated teethers of the late eighteenth and early nineteenth century are now treasured heirlooms.

Despite the enormous social and technological changes that have transformed the modern world, baby rattles and teethers have retained their functions. Whether they are made of simple straw basketry, plastic, or precious metal, baby rattles and teethers have continued to amuse, solace, and protect children today as they have throughout history.

Fig. 37
Homemade rattle of cloth and paper. Clown's head with bells attached mounted on a wooden stick. Date undetermined. Length: 8 inches. From the collection of Ada Ghiron Segal.

Fig. 38
Plastic rattle, U.S., c.1950. Alphabet rattle, probably part of a set, with two letters on each block and line drawings of nursery rhyme characters. Size: 2-inch cube with rounded corners.

Fig. 50
Reproduction rattle, U.S., c.1990.
Vermeil rattle in a fancy box designed
to look antique. Length: 3 inches.

Collecting: A Joy or an Obsession?

Getting Started

If you have ever collected anything at all, your story of how you got started will, no doubt, be very similar to this: An object catches your eye in an antique shop, or a museum, or on a friend's shelf. Perhaps you've never seen an "Ainu Mustache Lifter"—or whatever—before. The object intrigues you and your curiosity is piqued. When you eventually see something similar for sale, you buy it. Then you are motivated to look up its meaning or history or function. The first thing you buy may be a fake, a reproduction, or a tourist piece, but next time you are more careful, and before you know it, you are hooked on collecting.

Dr. Werner Muensterberger, himself a well-known collector of primitive art, has pointed out, in his book *Collecting: The Unruly Passion*, that a collecting urge often seizes people at a very young age, and those who succumb to it when they are children usually remain collectors throughout their lives. Indeed, he adds, collecting can become obsessive, taking up almost all of a collector's waking hours. His book gives several examples of this. It has even been known for a collector to embezzle his firm's funds for the sake of an addition to his collection!

How did some baby rattle collectors get started? One collector I know had been buying early American portraits, and one of the paintings he had showed a child with a rattle. Soon after he bought the painting, he came across a rattle in an antique shop that looked very much like the one in his picture. He bought it and began his rattle collection!

Another collector I know has a multitude of nieces and nephews. Each time a new baby arrived in the family, she searched for a suitable gift. On one of her quests, she discovered a reproduction of an antique rattle, and soon she was looking for originals for herself.

Other collectors tell similar stories. Pediatricians may receive a gift of a rattle from a child's grateful family, or a collector in another field may find a rattle that seems connected to his or her specialty and go on from there.

Collecting has started romances and caused divorces, and to be candid, divorces are more common. The dedicated collector, not to mention the obsessed one, can fill every nook and cranny of his or her home with the treasures that make up the collection!

Collecting is fun. Putting together an assemblage of objects which give pleasure and pride seems to satisfy some deep human instinct. Most children want to collect something at a very young age, whether it be stones, shells, or baseball cards. Some of them never give up the habit as adults, as Dr. Muensterberger has noted.

The "collector's bug" may even be in the genes. Recent research allows that there may be an "anxiety" gene, so why not a collector's gene as well? The passion to collect is certainly stronger in some people than in others, but even the most casual collector experiences the thrill of finding an unusual piece as well as the pleasure of displaying it. The fringe benefits of collecting include becoming an expert on a particular subject. Telling others about your hobby is very gratifying to the ego! Collecting baby rattles and teethers adds a heart-warming and even sentimental quality to the pursuit, for such objects can always be associated with the happy occasion of the birth of a new baby, even if it was a century or two ago. For the new collector, the whole world and its history offer an ample menu of delights.

How does one go about starting a baby rattle and teether collection? Let's assume that you have acquired your first rattle. Perhaps it is one you had as a child, or one you have retrieved from the family keepsakes. The first rule in any kind of collecting is to do your homework. Research is an integral part of every collector's arsenal of knowledge. The more you know, the fewer mistakes you will make.

There are many sources available for learning about rattles. Before making an investment in any field, the neophyte must first become familiar with the material in which he or she is interested. Finding out what rattles and teethers look like and how they looked in the past is the first step. Recognizing the various types of rattles and teethers, and their

Fig. 40
Miniature Painting, England, c.1830. The child is
holding a coral-and-bells of simple design. A lock
of hair is enclosed in the frame, so it is believed to
be a memorial piece. The grayish color of "the baby
with the old face," as some of these paintings were
called, may merely be the artist's lack of skill.
Artist unknown. Height: 2-3/4 inches.

dates and places of origin, can be an enormous
help when you are scouring the market for new
finds.

Start your research with your local museums.
Most art museums have baby rattles somewhere in
their collections. They may be among the antiquities, exhibited with musical instruments, in toy
sections, or mixed in with antique silver displays.
Ethnographic and natural history museums also
often show rattles in their cultural history exhibits.
If you are lucky enough to have a toy museum or a
doll museum near you, you will be sure to find
some rattles, teethers, and doll rattles there.

Paintings, prints, and miniatures in museums

are also wonderful places to trace the history of
rattles. Children have always been a prime subject
for painters, and children holding rattles or
teethers are depicted in some pictures. Miniature
portraits of children, on ivory or vellum, have been
made from the sixteenth century on. Although
most early miniatures were portraits of royalty and
were used to show the princes and princesses eligible for marriages, the young heirs stemming from
these unions were also painted. Later, miniature
paintings of their children were given as keepsakes
to fathers soon to be away at sea or at war, and
these too sometimes show rattles being held. Sadly,
some of these miniatures were *memento mori*,
picturing a child who had died. In some cases a
lock of the dead child's hair was placed inside the
frame (Fig. 40).

Museum treasures like these are an important
guide for the collector of antique rattles, because
the costume of the sitter and the date of the painting provide clues to the provenance of any rattles
you may find. For example, if a woman in a
portrait holding an infant is wearing an Empire-
style dress, you know that the child's rattle dates
from that period. Then, when you are looking at
rattles in a shop or show, you can place the date of
a similar style at 1800-1820. An off-the-shoulder
dress on a little girl identifies the date of the rattle
she is holding from the 1840-1850 period, when
such clothes were worn.

Often these portrait painters were anonymous
self-taught artists who went from town to town
offering to do portraits of children and families.
Some were more talented than others, with the
result that many portraits were of "babies with old
faces," where the painter couldn't get it quite right.
Their charm lies in their naïveté, and these "primi-
tives" are much sought after.

In many of these paintings, children are holding toys—hobby horses, dolls, hoops, flowers, or
bilboquets—but in a few, mainly in the portraits of
younger children, they are holding rattles. Unfortunately, there are many, many more toys, dogs, and
flowers than teethers and rattles.

Several books have been published on portraits
of children, and these may be more accessible to
the collector than museum paintings. Children's
books and books on toys and dolls can also provide
some background material on rattles and teethers.
The detail from a paper doll book (Fig. 41), shows
both a rattle and a teether. Because the date of
publication was 1908, any similar rattles or teethers
you may come across can be dated to that period.

Fig. 41
Paper Doll book, German, c.1908. Detail from a sheet of paper doll cut-outs showing a tin rattle and teether.

The Marketplace

Once a little knowledge about baby rattles has been gained, it is time to see what is out there in the marketplace. Becoming aware of the different kinds of rattles that appeal to you is the jumping off point for starting a new collection. Besides seeing what sort of rattles and teethers are being offered for sale, deciding what you are willing to pay for them must come into your calculations, too.

Where do you start to look for rattles? The most obvious sources are antique shows, toy and silver auctions, and antique shops. You must remember that in these places, the prices will be highest, because in effect the rattles have been pre-selected for you. Rattles can also turn up at country auctions or in estate sales. Make sure you look for them wherever old toys or children's books are being sold. Shops that sell international folk art often carry rattles from faraway places, and museum shops sometimes unload old toys, including rattles, and they also may produce authentic reproductions of antique rattles, especially at Christmas. Flea markets, street fairs, and garage sales offer more in the way of reasonably priced

Fig. 43
Minnie Mouse rattle, U.S., c.1930s. Authentic Disney head of stuffed cotton; has a cotton loop. Length: 5 inches.

objects. And don't ignore thrift shops and bazaars.

It would be nice to walk into an exclusive antique shop and plunk down several thousand dollars for a Georgian or Regency rattle in pristine condition with a famous maker's mark, but how can you collect baby rattles on a shoestring? The greatest pleasure comes from serendipity—the good luck of finding a treasure in an unexpected place. An aunt or cousin may have an old rattle from her forebears, or a box of toys in the attic may yield a find.

One of the greatest joys for a collector is to look for rattles while traveling. I have been lucky enough to have visited a great part of the world, and I have seldom come home without an addition or two for my collection. Searching for a specific category of object gives an extra focus to your travels, and you will always connect memories of that trip with the objects you bought.

Some years ago I made a surprising find in Paris in a shop that sold antique weapons. My husband and I were drawn by the window display and went in to inquire about an African knife that my husband was interested in. Just on the off-chance, I was inspired to ask if they had any baby rattles. Sure enough, the proprietor dug into a drawer and came up with a miniature gun, plated in heavy silver with a bell attached, and a whistle tip (Fig. 42). He dated it as mid-nineteenth century.

Fig. 42
Toy Gun rattle, France, mid-nineteenth century. Heavy silver plate. Style is reminiscent of a dueling pistol. Whistle tip, one silver bell. Length: 4 inches.

Even though little boys wore skirts then until they were out of diapers, machismo existed way back then! I paid a lot, but it is a star in my collection!

What You Should Expect to Pay

Rattles can cost anywhere from fifty cents, if you are lucky at a flea market, to several thousand dollars at a major silver auction. The asking prices for Georgian and Regency coral-and-bells have soared dramatically in the last few years. Depending on the condition and the name of the maker, examples in silver start at close to $1,000 and gold rattles and teethers can easily triple that figure or more. Mid- and late-Victorian silver or ivory rattles run considerably less, and early twentieth century ones are still in the bargain class. Old wood, tin, and celluloid rattles can be bought for less than $100, sometimes much less. Bakelite, on the other hand, is highly collectible and prices for Bakelite rattles often rival those of silver.

Some idea of present-day prices for different types of rattles may be suggested by my experiences in the past year. I found a cloth Minnie Mouse rattle from the 1930s for $12 (Fig. 43), a silver rattle from Taxco, Mexico, c.1950, at $39 (Fig. 44), and a Georgian gold and coral teether for $2,200—this was a special anniversary present (Fig. 45).

To be realistic, it is highly unlikely that you will find any silver rattle for fifty cents, but you might find an interesting old tin or celluloid one for not much more. When you are at an antique show or flea market, poke around among the toys but do not limit yourself to looking at toys alone. Rattles

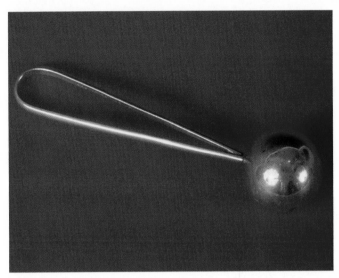

Fig. 44
Taxco rattle, Mexico, c. 1940–1950. Hollow silver ball with long silver loop handle. Marked "Taxco, Mexico." This unsigned example shows how the period's style was translated to baby rattles. Length: 3-5/8 inches.

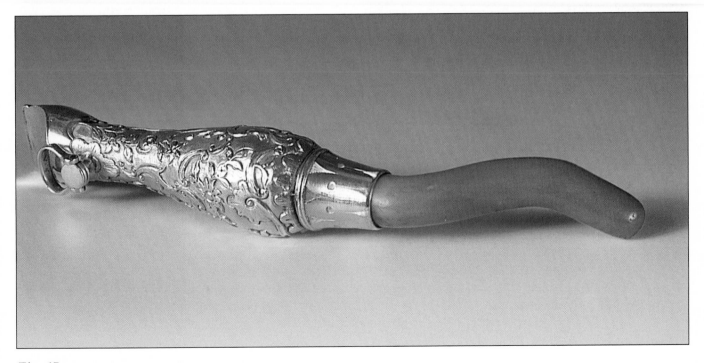

Fig. 45
Coral and Gold Teether, England, George II, 1775. Very fine brightwork, whistle tip, and a thick coral handle. Hallmark identifies Nicholas Dunee. Length: 5-1/2 inches.

Fig. 46
Victorian rattle, England, c.1875. George Unita rattle with a silver ring in place of a coral handle. Has a whistle tip. Length: 4 inches (without ring).

can be displayed mixed in with costume jewelry, flatware or with a jumble of "small silver," as the dealers call it, including silver bookmarks, cigar cutters, sewing accessories, and money clips.

If you become interested in antique rattles and teethers, you must be prepared to face some very stiff prices. Most gold and silver rattles from the Georgian and Regency period command astronomical prices today. Rattles and teethers in more moderate price ranges are still plentiful in the market. Late nineteenth and early twentieth century examples in silver, tin, ivory, and celluloid are not too difficult to find.

For those of you who want to collect miniatures and paintings which feature children and rattles and teethers, keep in mind that they are very expensive. An early nineteenth century American painting can sell for $20,000 or more, depending on its date and the fame of the artist. On the other hand, you may have a stroke of luck and find one for only a few hundred dollars! This is where your background knowledge will serve you well. British and American nineteenth century miniatures can

be found today in the $1,000 to $2,000 range. If the gods smile on you, you may find one for half that amount.

It is easy to see from this that rattles and teethers can be bought today in any price range. Whatever the cost, the dedicated collector always seems to be able to find the money for yet another purchase! Beginners must be cautious, though. Buying on impulse is an expensive way to pay for your education.

A Quick Lesson on Silver

If you decide to concentrate on collecting antique rattles, here are some words of caution: Silver rattles from the past present a difficult problem of authenticity. Until you are yourself an expert, trust in the dealer is a necessity. Although most dealers will be honest, and many of them started as collectors themselves, not all dealers are knowledgeable. Many tend to accept the word of the person they bought the object from without further investigation, so it pays to beware.

Not every piece of English or Continental silver is hallmarked, and even if it is, the marks can be difficult or impossible to decipher if they are worn away or have been poorly struck. American silver in the early days carried the maker's mark, and later almost all American silver was stamped "Sterling." The name of the manufacturer or its symbol is often included as well. It is a good idea to arm yourself with a magnifying glass or to borrow the dealer's loupe to inspect the marks yourself. Because you may be considering a real investment of money, you want to be sure you are getting just what you are paying for. Silver-plated rattles started to be made in the mid-nineteenth century, and sometimes their appearance can be deceptive. Dealers have a simple test to determine if the object is sterling. A list of books that can be used to identify silver marks is included in this book's bibliography.

It is very important to your collection to seek examples in the best possible condition. Novice collectors are tempted to buy incomplete or damaged rattles because they are usually less expensive. Condition affects the price sharply and also determines the resale value. And if you can get the original box, save it! This adds a lot to the value, too. Naturally, old rattles show signs of wear and tear and sometimes even the baby's teeth marks, and celluloid crushes, wood splinters, tin rusts, and cloth tatters! All of these imperfections determine the worth of the rattle.

As a rule, silver rattles tend to show less damage, for they were carefully handled family treasures to be used only on special occasions. The most elaborate rattles, like the coral-and-bells, were worn on a chain or chatelaine by the mother or nurse or attached to the child's waist by a ribbon. Nevertheless, silver rattles can be offered for sale in a distressed condition. They can be banged up or dented, or most often, lacking one or more of their original bells, a ring, or a handle.

Repairing or restoring old rattles is a tricky business. The original coral is often missing and it is not unusual to see it replaced with a piece of branch coral. This could never have been the original handle, because the sharp edges would have made it too dangerous for a baby to touch. As a general rule, the thicker and smoother the coral is, the older the piece. Crystal, agate, and carnelian were sometimes used as substitutes for coral, but these were the original handles, especially in Continental Europe where coral was scarce.

The silver bells are the first things to be lost on

Fig. 47
Lady with Furled Umbrella rattle, France, late nineteenth century. Silver with an ivory handle; the bells are missing. Height: 5 inches.

an antique rattle because they are very delicate and the loops attaching them to the rattle are fragile. It is virtually impossible to replace Georgian and Regency period silver bells with authentic ones unless the dealer cannibalizes a damaged rattle for its parts. This is called "marrying" and is a common practice among dealers in antique silver. Fig. 46 is a George Unita rattle, dated about 1875, where the coral is missing and a large silver ring

was fastened to the original holder. It still might amuse the baby, but the piece has lost its place as an authentic late Victorian rattle, and its value has decreased accordingly. Marrying is also used to give an antique piece more interest. Old watches have their faces lifted by the substitution of a beautifully painted face of the same period. In baby rattles, it happens too. Fig. 47 is a French rattle from the late nineteenth century. The figure is holding a furled umbrella. She is missing several bells from her skirt. In Fig. 48, the bells have been replaced and an open umbrella with bells has been added. On close examination, this is easy to detect, because the top does not exactly fit!

Silver and silver-plated rattles, beginning with the advent of machine pressing and stamping in the mid-nineteenth century, came with mother-of-pearl or ivory teething rings or handles. These were easily lost or broken, but the rings are not too difficult to find. The handle of a flatware butter knife or salad fork from the same period as the rattle will serve as a substitute for the original, because many rattles were manufactured by makers of cutlery.

Fig. 48
Lady with Open Umbrella rattle, France, late nineteenth century. This is the same casting as Fig. 47, but with an open umbrella. Bells were added to the umbrella and skirt. Overall length: 7 inches.

Fig. 49
Dumbbell rattle, France, c.1900. Silver rattle with lightly incised striped pattern. Has a silver chain and an ivory ring. Shown in its original box. Length: 3-1/2 inches.

Fig. 51
Reproduction rattle, U.S., c.1980s. Silver. Faithful reproduction of an antique Spanish spinner rattle.
Offered in the Cartier Christmas Catalogue 1984. Length: 6 inches.

As with all antiques, the value of a rattle of whatever vintage diminishes with the amount of restoration and repair it has undergone. Inspect your purchase carefully and always make sure to ask the dealer to indicate any areas that are not original. Old rattles are sometimes resilvered, leaving them shiny and bright. It is up to you to decide if you prefer that particular finish to the "use patina" that old silver acquires and that many collectors cherish.

There are some other things to be aware of when you start a rattle collection. Rattles are so popular as gifts today that a whole industry has arisen to make reproductions! Fig. 49 is a silver dumbbell from France in its original gift box, dating from about 1900. Fig. 50 is a very similar design in vermeil, offered by a doll catalogue company just a few years ago. Fig. 51 is a very good reproduction of an antique Spanish rattle which appeared in the Christmas catalogue of Cartier in the 1980s. These examples are perfectly legitimate, because they were clearly marked as reproductions. But what about out-and-out fakes?

What exactly is a fake? A fake is anything sold to you as something it is not. For the inexperienced collector there is much to learn about the subterfuges used by unscrupulous dealers to trap the unwary. The technique of marrying elements from damaged rattles to make a complete one creates a fake if it is offered to you as a complete original. Lopping off fifty years or more from the actual age of the rattle is another ploy. Many late-Victorian rattles resemble or were based on Georgian models, and naturally the earlier date commands a much higher price. Silver plate sold as sterling may also be considered a fake, and so is a reproduction, if it is not clearly presented as such.

A friend recently brought me a beautiful Humpty-Dumpty rattle with a mother-of-pearl handle. He had found it in a London flea market for twenty pounds (about $35). It was marked with the inscription "Virginia Hayes, 1848." I couldn't believe it was real at that price (Fig. 52).

In looking over my notes, I found an identical rattle featured in an article in the *Antique Reproduction Newsletter* of February 1995. It explained that the reproductions were made of a chrome-plated heavy metal, cast from an original silver rattle. One of these reproductions was my friend's proud find, of course. The punchline of the story is that an advertisement in the *Maine Antiques Digest* recently offered the same rattle as an original for $175! That would be a very good price for a real Victorian rattle, but was very high for a copy. We must assume that the dealer selling the rattle was fooled, too.

Be suspicious if a silver rattle is priced far too low for the going rate. Dealers may not deliberately cheat you, but as I've noted before, they do not always do their homework. They are all too ready to believe that it was they themselves who got the bargain when they bought the piece.

Fig. 52
Reproduction rattle, England, 1990s. Chrome over base metal. Humpty-Dumpty cast from an original Victorian rattle. Inscription reads "Virginia Hayes, 1848." Length: 5 inches.

The first two rattles I bought, the ones from Spain I have mentioned before, were outright fakes! They may have been cast from antique originals, or merely based on them, but they were sold to me as authentic. Now that I have learned a lot more about rattles, I can see where they differ from real ones. Fig. 53, the sea monster, is both larger and heavier than a genuine eighteenth century rattle; it has also been gold-plated, a rarity for that type of rattle. Fig. 54, the clown, is also heavier than a real rattle of the early twentieth century would be. I was too inexperienced to be wary of the low price!

Excellent reproductions of rattles in sterling silver are being made today in Spain and the Netherlands, and, I suspect, in other countries as well. The silver mark on such rattles is usually what confuses the unwary buyer. These reproductions are often sold in baby's clothing stores and in museum shops, and they are clearly marked for what they are.

When you are out looking for rattles, you will find that there are many objects for sale which look like baby rattles but which were intended for another use. Small musical instruments like tambourines (which have also been used as models for baby rattles), or like maracas, do not qualify as baby rattles. Neither do party favors and New Year's Eve noisemakers, although they may have bells and ribbons and clappers. Beekeeper's rattles (used to distract bees when they were swarming) and cowbells may or may not have been used to amuse children, but that was certainly not their primary function. And the rattles that Shamans and medicine men have used for tribal purposes throughout the world cannot be thought of as baby rattles. Dealers can have very lively imaginations when they are trying to sell you something!

Collecting Patterns

After you have accumulated a few rattles, a pattern will begin to emerge that indicates what sort of collector you will turn out to be. There are collectors who want one (or more) of every kind of rattle and teether that they can find. Others, who are more selective, concentrate on only one area, style, or period.

Both modes have their advantages. Collectors who take the broader view have a much wider field to choose from, and their options are only limited by their pocketbooks and the access they have to a variety of sources. The drawback to this sort of collection is that it is inclined to lack focus and may wind up a hodgepodge of unrelated objects. Collectors in this category must be constantly on the lookout for examples that fill in the gaps in their collection.

The specialized collection has its merits, too. A group of objects, in the same style or from the same place makes a much stronger aesthetic statement. Also it is probably easier to build a collection and do more extensive research on a specific type of rattle than to have a bit of everything. To limit one's collection to one area demands discipline and commitment, which may be difficult to maintain in the face of the many temptations in the market-place. And there is no doubt that a refined and cohesive collection will turn out to have a greater value should you ever decide to dispose of it. Specialized collectors still have a wide choice in the type of rattle they collect. They may opt for rattles from antiquity or primitive and folk art pieces. If their pockets are deep enough, they can confine themselves to coral-and-bells rattles. Rattles with an animal theme or character collectibles, or only tin or celluloid rattles could be another path to follow. Rattles exist in so many forms that there are plenty of them out there for everyone. The chief disadvantage of the specialized collection is that dealers will usually raise their prices when they find a unique or rare piece that you simply must have!

You might imagine, for example, that rattles from antiquity would be next to impossible to find. Surprisingly, they turn up at auctions fairly often. And don't overlook dealers who handle artifacts from ancient Greece and Rome, India, the Near East, Egypt, and pre-Columbian America. Once the word gets around that you are interested in a certain item, you'd be amazed at what dealers can find for you.

The competition for rattles in the market is quite extensive. Grandparents and godparents buy them for new babies, and collectors of infantilia, such as baby feeders and pap spoons, are tempted by the baby rattles and teethers too. Doll fanciers are always looking for accessories, and doll rattles in scale with their dolls or doll houses are a true find for them. There are also the people who are interested in character collectibles like Mickey Mouse, Santa Claus, or Kewpie dolls. Those who collect specific animals also impinge on the rattle field. There are many other areas of collecting where rattles may appeal to collectors, like tin toys, American Indian material, Pennsylvania Dutch objects and folk art to name but a few. Bell collectors usually have a few rattles, and, of course, so do collectors of antique silver, Art Nouveau, and Art Deco.

Despite all of this, collecting baby rattles and teethers is still a relatively wide-open field. Because of their universal use, there is no shortage of interesting and beautiful examples for the new collector. If you can concentrate on an area that is still open, many kinds of rattles are still available at reasonable prices. Folk art rattles, Art Nouveau and Art Deco, and American and British rattles of the late nineteenth century and Pre-World War I periods now are in plentiful supply. Celluloid objects are increasing in value as well, as are toys of tin,

Fig. 53
Sea Monster rattle, Spain, 1980s, Vermeil. Modern adaptation of an eighteenth century Spanish example with a whistle tip and a full set of bells. Length: 6 inches.

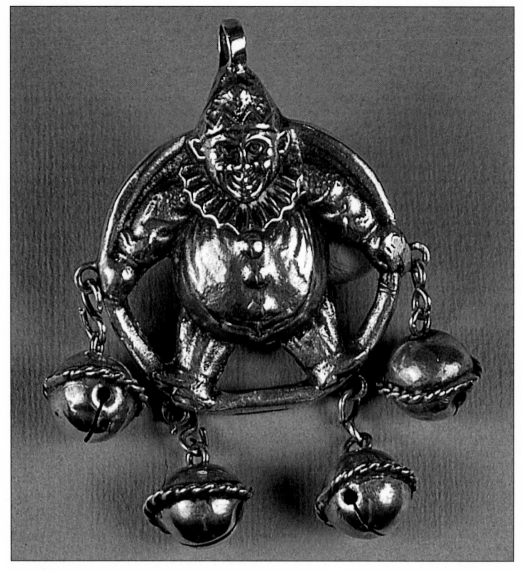

Fig. 54
Reproduction rattle,
Spain, 1980. Heavy
silver clown; reproduc-
tion of an early twenti-
eth century rattle (poor
casting). Has a complete
set of bells, but the ring
is missing. Diameter: 2-
3/4 inches.

mother-of-pearl, and pre-embargo ivory. Another direction to consider is to choose one geographical location and stay with the rattles that originate there. Whatever way you go is the right way, as long as it gives you pleasure and excitement!

Remember that present-day rattles need not be step-children in a collection. It is interesting to see the continuity of forms which date back hundreds of years still being made today. Drum shapes, dumbbells, balls, and spinners continue to appeal to children, even if they are made of plastic. In addition, many modern craftsmen are making unique pieces, usually in wood, where the shapes and textures of the rattles are a pleasure to look at and hold. And today's popular children's icons, like Kermit the Frog and Barney the Dinosaur, will surely join Donald Duck and Mickey Mouse as the character collectibles of the future. Only the collector's imagination can limit what he or she may choose to collect! Who would have thought forty years ago that such esoteric or common objects as

barbed wire or Coca-Cola bottles would have hordes of enthusiastic fans buying them up?

So, whether you collect treasures or trifles, pieces of antiquity or modern-day items, you will find collecting baby rattles and teethers an absorbing and gratifying hobby.

Who Collects Rattles and Teethers?

Oddly enough, most of the serious collectors of baby rattles and teethers have been men. But perhaps this is not so surprising, because up to very recent times, men most often had control of a family's disposable income. Among the collectors I know personally there are three male pediatricians whose collections began with a gift from a child's parents.

The two largest collections in the world belonged to two European gentlemen: Ides Cammaert of Brussels and Heinz Kejyser of Amsterdam. They were generous enough to bequeath their collections to public institutions.

Five hundred of Ides Cammaert's rattles have been put on display in a small private museum, Bibliothek Wittockiana, maintained by his family in Tervuren, a suburb of Brussels, and may be visited by appointment. A small illustrated catalogue in French and Flemish with highlights of the collection is listed in this book's bibliography. The remainder of his collection including paintings and prints has been distributed among family members.

Heinz Kejyser had more than twelve hundred rattles in his collection (even he was not sure of the exact number) plus a host of related objects including paintings, prints, and firescreens. Several items in the collection dated back to the fifteenth century. He also had several sets of gold rattles and feeding spoons in their original presentation boxes. He was kind enough to take them out of the vault for me to see when I visited him. His collection is at present being installed in a new museum in southern Holland that will be devoted to children.

The late Nathaniel Spear of New York was primarily a collector of bells and author of a definitive book on the subject, but he had many baby rattles in his collection. I was fortunate enough to see the collection on a number of occasions, and had the opportunity to buy some of his rattles when they came up at auction. Most of Mr. Spear's formidable bell collection has been left to the Metropolitan Museum in New York.

Getting in Touch with Other Collectors

As of this writing no club or newsletter has been formed for collectors of baby rattles. So how do you get in touch with other collectors?

First there are other well-established clubs which deal with rattle-related objects. For example there is a Bell Collector's Club and many of its members have rattles in their collections. There is also a newsletter for collectors of baby bottles and feeders whose readership may include rattle collectors. *The Directory of Clubs and Associations* is the best source for locating these clubs. The address is included in the bibliography following this text, and your library is sure to have a copy in the reference department.

In addition, there are many small weekly, bi-weekly, and monthly newspapers dealing with antiques and collectibles where you can run an advertisement for rattles or for information on other collectors in their classified sections. These ads can bring rewarding results, for you will hear from dealers you could not otherwise reach. Many of these papers are given away free at antique shows and antique malls. Usually these papers also have letter columns where you may write for information regarding the identification of a piece. The wider you cast your net for information, the better the chances for finding out more about rattles.

Cataloguing Your Collection

Some people enjoy paper work and take pleasure in keeping meticulous records. Others of us stuff everything into shoe boxes and shopping bags and worry about sorting things out at some other time. However, when it comes to cataloguing your collection, it is absolutely essential to keep thorough and up-to-date records of everything you own. As time goes by and your collection grows, it is easy to forget where you bought an object, from whom you got it, and what you paid. Consequently, it is a very good idea to get all of the facts written down when your purchase is new and the information is fresh in your mind.

There are some fairly simple rules to follow when you are establishing a catalogue for a new collection. If these practices become routine at the beginning, they will save you a lot of work later on.

First, you must choose the most convenient way to keep records. Some collectors use 3" x 5" index cards, some use a small notebook, and others use a computer. Second, decide on a numbering and classification system for the collection. You have a variety of options. I believe the simplest way of keeping a catalogue is to list the rattles in chronological order of purchase, followed by the identification number of the object, as follows:
1997. 1: Baby Rattle, American, etc.
This is the method used by most museums. However, this system will make looking up information more difficult as the number of objects in your collection expands. Cross references are also used by museums, but this involves a whole other set of entries.

In general, classifications tend to focus either on the place of origin of the object or the material it is made of. In the first instance, where the place of origin is used, your entry would begin something like this:
Number 1: American rattle, silver, etc.
On the other hand, if your classification is based on material, your entry would read:
Number 1: Silver rattle, American, etc.

Fig. 55
Bell rattle, U.S., c.1910–1920.
Silver bell with a mother-of-
pearl ring. Embossed figure
of a child reaching for the
moon. It is inscribed "Baby
Secrets" on the front. Height
1-3/4 inches.

One other type of classification is worth mentioning. If your collection is the all-inclusive kind, you may want to list your rattles by the time period in which they originated:

Number 1: 1910-1920, silver rattle, American, etc.

What other data must be included with each entry? For each rattle in your collection, you should have somewhere in your records the place and date of purchase plus the name of the dealer or source. In addition, you should include the purchase price and the present value if it differs from the amount you paid. To the value, you must add the cost of any repair or restoration you have had done, and the cost of a professional photograph if you have had one taken. Noting whether you have the original box the rattle came in is also important because it will add greatly to the value. If you can identify the date the piece was made, and the place and maker, that, too, must be part of the catalogue, with the size and descriptions. To investigate the current value of a piece, a little research is required on your part. You can price similar rattles at dealers and antique shows, or in auction catalogues. And, if the identical rattle or one very close to it has been illustrated in a book or in an advertisement, that information should be added as well.

Here is a sample of what one of my note cards looks like (Fig. 55):

RA 1 (American)
Small silver bell with clapper, 2-1/4" x 2-1/4"
Circa 1910-1920; price: $27.50
Antiques Mall, St. Pete., FL 1996
Embossed design of baby reaching for moon
Inscribed "Baby Secrets" on front
Hallmark on back with symbol of Weber Co.
Stamped "Sterling" on back and loop
Mother-of-pearl ring

It may also be helpful to start a folder or file to keep any other information you can find about rattles. These might be museum postcards of paintings of children with rattles, clippings from newspapers or magazines, or advertisements in the antique press. Rattles for sale or auction appear quite often in the trade papers, and most vendors and auction houses are happy to give you the price or estimate if it is not listed. Be sure to mark your clippings with the date and the source, for these provide an excellent guide to current market prices of rattles you own or may consider buying in the future. Not only expensive rattles are offered in these publications. Tin, celluloid, and wooden rattles turn up along with the antique silver ones.

It is also wise to save all of your receipts and any correspondence you receive from dealers and other collectors. These are all very good references to have on hand when you are contemplating a major purchase, swap, or sale.

Although all of this may seem a lot of work, having truly complete records, even on your lesser rattles and teethers, will pay off handsomely if some of your rattles are chosen for a show or publication and especially if you should ever want to trade or sell part of your collection. The side benefit is that you are learning more and more about rattles with each addition to your collection.

Lights! Camera! Action!: Photographing Your Rattles

After your rattle catalogue is complete, the next step for a new collector is to consider photography. Whether you hire a professional or do it yourself is up to you. When you have already labeled, described, and classified your rattles and teethers, why are photographs important?

There are several reasons for having good, clear pictures of all of your pieces, even the less valuable ones. Photographs are necessary should you ever want to trade or sell your rattles, and they are essential for advertisements and for correspondence with other collectors. Also, if a piece of yours is chosen for an exhibition or book, you will have the picture ready. And, perhaps most importantly, your insurance company will demand photographs when covering your most expensive rattles.

Displaying Your Rattles: Showing Off or Shutting Away?

After you have started a collection of baby rattles and teethers, what is the best way for you to preserve, protect, and display them?

It's a natural human impulse to show the treasures you've acquired to your friends, but displaying small, delicate objects to their best advantage is a difficult task. They collect dust, silver tarnishes quickly, and the universal appeal of rattles is a temptation to sticky fingers in both senses of the words.

Collectors have found both conventional and inventive ways to install their pieces attractively. Corner cabinets, traditional what-nots, and knick-knack shelves harmonize with most decoration schemes and they are available in modern versions as well as traditional styles.

Here are some other options to consider: A glass-topped coffee table with a shelf beneath is a handsome and practical way to show silver rattles. Putting rattles on shallow bookshelves is often a route selected by collectors. There are even tiny strip lights on the market which can be affixed to the shelf above to highlight the rattles. Commercial jewelry display cases of glass, wood, or Lucite can be hung on the wall or be free-standing. These were designed to showcase small pieces, and many have interior lighting. Second-hand ones are not too hard to find at flea markets and thrift shops. Sometimes these cases are advertised in the classified section of newspapers that feature collectibles.

Shadow boxes hung on the wall like paintings are also popular for displaying small objects like rattles. Lit from within, the shadow boxes can enhance the importance of even your smallest rattles. Using fancy boxes for rattles is the choice of many collectors. They can be part of a room's decor. Japanese *tansu*, small chests of drawers that can stand on a table or desk, are beautiful works of art in themselves. Their many little drawers can hold your most precious rattles safely. The rattles can be kept in silver cloth or sealed plastic bags to protect them from pollution and tarnishing, but can still easily be taken out to show.

For rattles and teethers of lesser value and less fragility than the rare coral-and-bells, other arrangements can be made which are much less expensive. For example, one collector hung celluloid, ivory, and tin rattles on bright-colored satin ribbons in a very original way on a nursery wall. The rattles were out of the reach of the baby, of course!

Paintings and prints that show babies with rattles or teethers can be hung near your rattle display, if there is wall space available. The pictures constitute an impressive background for the collection, especially for guests who are unfamiliar with the whole field.

How you display your collection depends entirely on the amount of space you have, and on how much you are willing to invest in showing the rattles. As your collection expands, if you have limited space you may have to have revolving exhibitions, with the newest rattles taking pride of place on the shelves. If necessary, your other rattles can go back to shoe boxes under the bed!

However you choose to display your rattles and teethers, your collection deserves a handsome

Fig. 65
Oil painting, U.S., 1824. The little girl is carrying a classic coral-and-bells silver rattle. Artist unknown. Photograph coutesy of Marguerite Riordan

American Rattles and Teethers: From Puritans to Plastic

For more than a thousand years rattles and teethers have enjoyed a rich and diverse history all over the western hemisphere. This is readily evident when one considers the evolution of their forms, materials, and functions that range from the early tribal objects to the mass-produced rattles and teethers that are so common today.

From Alaska to Tierra del Fuego shaman's rattles were used for ceremonial purposes since the earliest times. In the United States and Canada rattles appeared in Native American curing, birth, and funeral rites, and as an imprecation to the gods for rain and good crops. But rattles were also used for non-ceremonial purposes. For example, the Eskimos employed rattles to lure seals from the water.

Native American rattles were made of shells, animal teeth and nails, wood, and turtle shells. Some were decorated with feathers or beads, or painted with symbolic designs. Other fetish material, of iconic significance to the tribe, was frequently added as well (Fig. 56).

Babies, too, had their rattles. Archaeologists have found small clay animal figures which rattle in the remains of the Casas Grandes culture of Arizona and New Mexico, dating from twelfth to fourteenth century A.D. (Fig. 57). Baby rattles have also been discovered in other early cultures in the area. Like the rattles used for religious purposes, baby rattles varied in style and materials with the ecologi-

cal and economic structure of a particular culture. In the northeast woodlands, babies had maple sugar teethers, while Eskimo babies got pieces of blubber to soothe them. Some patterns, however, do emerge.

From Alaska to Florida, Native American babies were carried in cradle-boards, called *hi-ka-tole* by the Pueblo peoples, and *dikona-gon* by the Plains Indians. The cradle-boards were constructed of a flat or slightly concave piece of wood about two feet high and fifteen inches across. This was surmounted by a bent wooden hoop attached to the cradle-board at right angles with wooden pegs. This protected the baby's head if the cradle-board fell. Sometimes a footrest was added at the bottom. The infant was wrapped in cloth or skins, tightly secured with its arms inside.

Amulets were hung on the head loop together with small toys and rattles (Fig. 58). The belief was that these charms formed a spider's web to keep harm away from the child. When the baby was a little older, it could free its arms and play with these objects. Cradle charms and rattles were made of tiny birch bark cones, animal bones, or small beaded bags containing the navel cord and other materials. These charms were also sewn on children's blankets, leggings, and other clothing.

The cradle-board was a safe and efficient way to transport the baby on its mother's back, or to hang on a tree away from small animals. It could also be easily carried on horseback or in a canoe. Apparently, the children liked the cradle-boards because they clamored to return to it when they were tired. It is even referred to in some tribes as the "third mother."

Rattles and teethers would appear to have been abandoned when babyhood was outgrown. At this point in a child's life in these Native American societies, toys

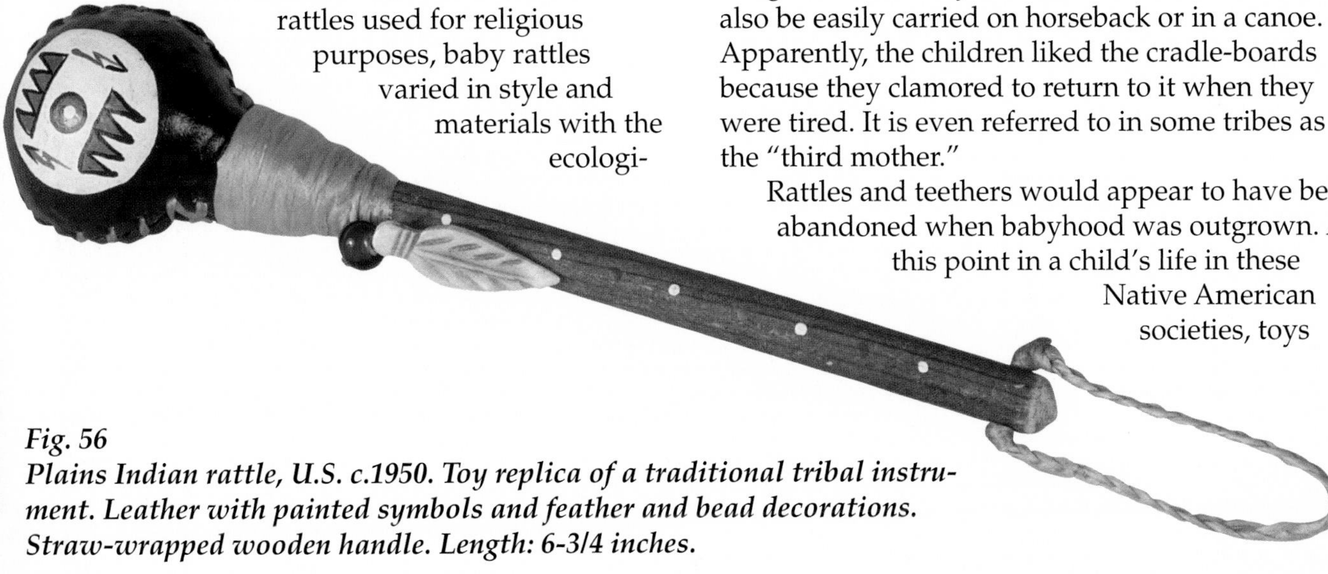

Fig. 56
Plains Indian rattle, U.S. c.1950. Toy replica of a traditional tribal instrument. Leather with painted symbols and feather and bead decorations. Straw-wrapped wooden handle. Length: 6-3/4 inches.

Fig. 57
Pre-Columbian baby rattle, Casas Grandes
culture, southwest U.S., c. twelfth to fourteenth
century A.D. Terra-cotta bird form with poly-
chrome design. Height: 2-7/8 inches.

became teaching tools. Skills and techniques were taught that would prepare the child for adult responsibilities. At a very young age, children were given small replicas of the objects they would use later on. Miniature canoes, bows and arrows, and toy horses were given to boys, while girls received needles, beads, and dolls to ready them for the tasks ahead.

Today, the Hopi and Navajo tribes of the American Southwest still observe many of their ancient ceremonies using rattles. Some of these are made in miniature for tourists' children. In the souvenir shops of New Mexico, the ancient symbols are used to decorate modern silver dumbbell rattles (Fig. 59).

When the Puritans arrived in the New World in the early seventeenth century, they brought with them their strict Calvinist ideas of child-raising. Children were considered to be born in sin, and were to be treated as small adults. Prayer and work

were the only paths to salvation. New England's stony soil and bitter winter weather could only have added to the grimness of their lives. Frivolity was frowned upon, and sumptuary laws were passed that limited expenditure on luxuries on the grounds of morality. Even Christmas was celebrated as a solemn and somber occasion. Play for children was an unknown concept.

Because infant mortality was one of the great scourges of the time, superstitious beliefs in curing and preventing childhood illness held sway. Disease was thought to be caused by "sortilege" or witchcraft, and drastic measures were taken to break evil spells. Trafficking in counter-charms, which rattles were considered to be, was almost as great a sin as witchcraft. In this society, trinkets like expensive baby rattles had no place, but babies must have had some sort of teether of wood, cloth, or other material, and some secret amulets as well. None of these seem to have survived, though.

These restrictions on luxuries did not apply to the settlers in the Dutch Colonies in New York in

Fig. 58
Print of Ojibway mother and child, showing
cradle board with amulets hung on hoop.

the late seventeenth century. Motivated by commerce, rather than religious beliefs, prosperous merchants were able to indulge themselves and their families with the same comforts they had left behind in Holland. Among the many kinds of imported goods that made their way to port of New York were baby rattles and teethers. A fine example of this is the gold pap spoon with two bells attached, which was made for a baby in the DePeyster family in 1695 (Fig. 60). This piece is a variation of a style popular in Holland at the time, which was usually made of lesser materials. American-made gold rattles of this period can be seen in the collections of Yale University and the Boston Museum. The Metropolitan Museum in New York has a gold coral-and-bells rattle with a thick coral handle, made by Nicholas Roosevelt in New York in 1735 (Fig. 61). Among the other crafts-men who made baby rattles and teethers in the late 1700s were Daniel Fueter and Eilias Pilltreau. Almost all of the examples of gold rattles of this time still existing were made in New York.

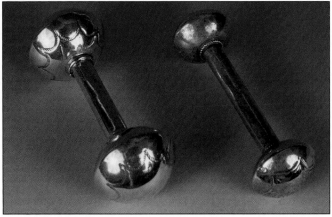

Fig. 59
Two Navajo rattles, southwest U.S., c.1960-1980. Dumbbell-shaped rattles with tribal designs engraved on the ends. Marked "sterling."Length: 3-1/2 inches each.

Information about baby rattles and teethers in the Colonial Period in America is limited to adver-tisements in newspapers of the time and portraits of children with rattles—the sons and daughters of the upper classes. British settlers in Boston, Philadelphia, New York, and Charleston developed a wealthy society based on trade. They imported furniture, jewelry, and tea in exchange for cotton, fur, and tobacco.

Baby rattles, surprisingly, seemed to be quite an important item, judging by the number of adver-tisements that offered them for sale or at auction in the newspapers of the larger cities. Some of these ads appeared as early as 1710. There was even a notice printed in the South Carolina Gazette in 1738 of the theft of a "Whistle, coral and chain"!

Obviously, these expensive toys had value as a status symbol, although the belief in the magic properties of coral continued for another century. At the same time, "anodyne necklaces," first mentioned by the Roman physician Orabasius in the fifth century, were still being imported into the Colonies in the mid-1700s. They consisted of beads carved of hard wood, such as peony wood, and were used as teethers.

Coral-and-bells rattles and teethers continued to be imported even after the American Revolution, but by then, gold- and silversmiths were well-established in the Colonies. It is interesting to note that the objects made in the thriving cities reflected the character of each place. Boston furniture and decoration, silver objects included, were restrained in design, while sturdy Dutch influence prevailed in New York, and Philadelphia displayed a more exuberant taste.

Fig. 60
Dutch Colonial pap spoon, New York, c.1660. This gold spoon has two attached bells. Length: 7-1/4 inches.

Trading vessels coming into the major ports were eagerly awaited by children, for their cargoes often brought toys not available at home. There is a story about Benjamin Franklin, aged seven in 1713, making his way to Boston's harbor to meet one of these ships. On the way he spent his pennies on a bad bargain, a "whistle," with another boy. Presumably, he never made a bad bargain again!

Skilled craftsmen throughout the Colonies made silver pepperpots, sugar tongs, spoons, snuffboxes, tea and coffee services, and, of course, baby rattles and teethers. Designs were directly derived from the English prototypes. In Boston, Paul Revere and his son produced silver-and-coral teethers and rattles in the late 1770s (Fig. 62). A record exists of Martha Washington's purchase of a silver coral-and-bells for her first grandson in 1791. She paid twenty-five dollars for it, an enormous sum in those days. Unfortunately, the maker's name and the present whereabouts of the piece remain unknown.

Portraits of children of wealthy families were painted in America, following a tradition long followed in Europe, by artists who had been trained abroad. Later, self-taught or American-trained artists would take their place. Quite often, these children in the portraits were shown with rattles, perhaps exhibiting a family treasure. Both professional and untutored artists traveled from town to town, creating family portraits, children's portraits, and miniatures. Sometimes these "limners," as these itinerant painters were called, would bring with them pre-painted canvases, complete except for the faces and hands. These would be painted *in situ* at the family home, and the favorite object or symbolic professional item, or a Bible, would be added with the hands. Perhaps rattles were among the items brought by the painter.

Fig. 61
Colonial U.S. rattle, New York, c.1750. Gold with engraved scroll decoration and thick coral handle, original bells, whistle tip. Made by Nicholas Roosevelt. Length 6-1/4 inches. Courtesy the Metropolitan Museum of Art, New York, Rogers Fund, 1947.

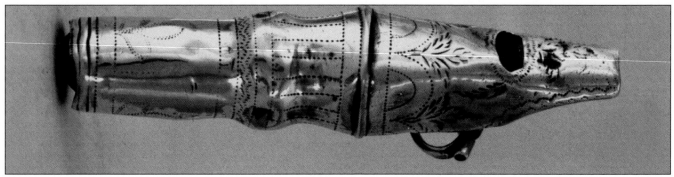

Fig. 62
Colonial U.S. teether, Boston, 1775. Embossed silver with whistle tip. The coral handle is missing. Made by Paul Revere II. Length: 6-1/8 inches. Courtesy the Museum of Fine Arts, Boston.

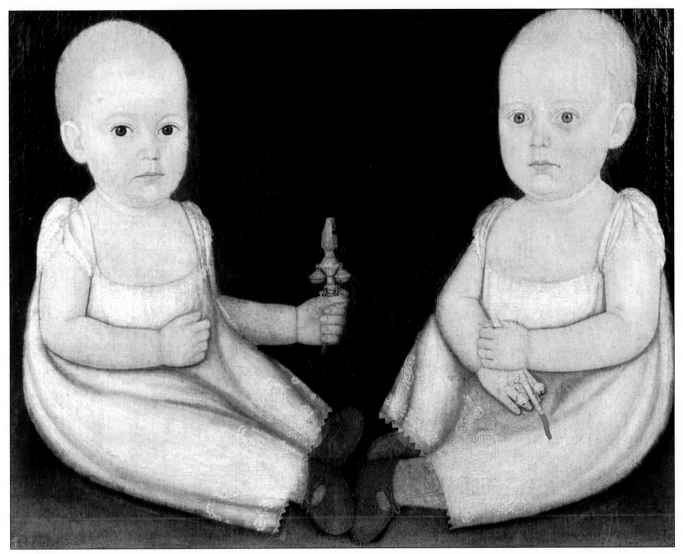

Fig. 63
Oil Painting, U.S., c.1810. Portrait of twins, each holding a coral-and-bells rattle, probably silver.
Artist, sitters, and present whereabouts unknown. Width: 22-1/2 inches; height: 20-1/4 inches.

By the 1830s, the popularity of coral-and-bells rattles had faded in the United States, and those that were being made were simpler and lighter, with thinner coral sticks. The tin and wicker rattles which succeeded them can be seen in the children's portraits of this era (Fig. 63, 64, 65, 66, 67, and 68). Among the better known New England artists were Ammi Phillips and the Peale family, but many lovely paintings are unsigned and the sitter is unknown. The charm of the children can be seen in all of them, though.

The study of these paintings and miniatures is important to a collector. From the costume and the style of the rattle or teether, and the date of the painting, if given, the age and provenance of a rattle you may be offered for sale can be determined. Paintings like these can be seen in many museum collections, and in some of the books mentioned in the bibliography that follows this text.

The Quaker settlements in the New World were somewhat more lenient in their child-rearing methods than the early New England colonists, and as time went on, more relaxed attitudes toward raising children were adopted throughout America. Religion was still a prominent part of life, and there were special "Sunday toys" permitted. These were usually based on Bible stories. The most popular was Noah's Ark with its pairs of animals. Hand-carved and painted sets of these are rare and valuable now.

The Pennsylvania Dutch community has also contributed to the lore of baby rattles. In the early part of the nineteenth century, small red clay

Fig. 64
Oil painting, U.S. c.1835-1840. Portrait of a young child carrying twisted straw rattle. It is difficult to decide if it is a boy or a girl, because both could wear dresses in any color at the time. Shown in its original frame. Height: 25-1/2 inches; Width: 22 inches.

Fig. 66
Oil Painting, U.S., c.1830. Double portrait of Mrs. Christopher Tompkins Estes and her son. The boy is holding a coral stick with bells attached. Artist unknown. Photograph courtesy of Marguerite Riordan.

Fig. 67
Watercolor painting, U.S. c.1830. Portrait of Charles William Marsh, attributed to Edwin Plummer (1802-1880). The child is holding a mallet-shaped rattle, possibly made of tin. From the collection of Raymond and Susan Egan, courtesy David A. Schorsch, New York.

*Fig. 69
Scrimshaw teethers, U.S., New England, c.1850s. Whalebone teething sticks, lightly incised. Meant to be hung across cradle where they could jingle or be pulled down by the baby. Length of each: 4-1/2 inches.*

rattles, some with whistles, were made there. They took the form of familiar barnyard animals and were painted and finished with a redware glaze. A few of these rattles were recently offered at auction for $500 to $2,000 each!

In the Lancaster, Pennsylvania, area, another custom arose which seems to be unique to that locale. In celebration of a couple's tenth wedding anniversary, gifts of tin were given. Gargantuan hats, huge shoes, monster-size coffeepots, and other items of tin on that scale, including baby rattles, were presented. An enormous tin baby rattle in a mallet shape turned up recently at an antique show for $850.

Other forms of rattles and teethers—which were until that time known as wissels, corals, baby-bells, or gumsticks—took shape in the first half of the nineteenth century. The New England whaling trade sent sailors away on long sea voyages. With time on their hands, they created objects of whalebone or ivory for the folks at home. Cribbage boards, pie-cutters, and swifts (yarn winders) were popular items, and teethers, rattles, and crib toys were made as well. This genre of folk art has come to be known as "scrimshaw" and is prized by collectors today (Fig. 69, 70, 71, 72, and 73).

Tin toys appeared on the market in the early 1830s, as can be seen in some children's portraits. Whistles and rattles in molded or pressed tin, often painted, were available in abundance from the middle of the nineteenth century. Tin mallets or drum shapes were the most common, but other

*Fig. 68
Miniature painting, U.S., c.1840. The little girl is holding a silver coral-and-bells rattle of traditional style. 3-1/2 inches high by 2-1/2 inches wide. Artist unknown.*

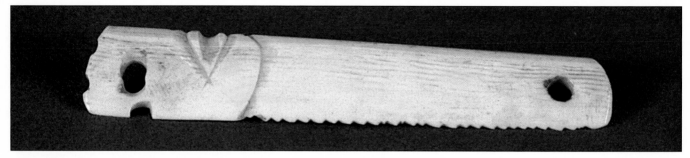

Fig. 70
Scrimshaw teether, U.S., New England, c.1850s. Ivory or bone carved in the shape of a saw. This may have been part of a set similar to Fig. 69. Length: 3-3/4 inches.

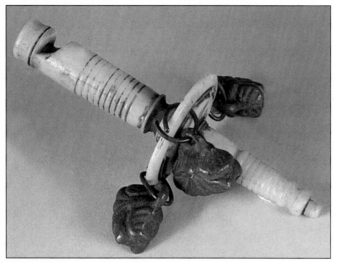

Fig. 71
Scrimshaw rattle, U.S., mid-nineteenth century. Carved whalebone stem with whistle tip. The pewter bells are unusual, although pewter was commonly used for household articles. Length: 3 inches. From the collection of Ada Ghiron Segal.

Fig. 72
Scrimshaw rattle, U.S., mid-nineteenth century. Ivory or whalebone mallet-shaped rattle with carved handle. Length: 4-1/2 inches.

Fig. 73
Scrimshaw rattle, U.S., mid-nineteenth century, Sag Harbor, New York. Ivory or whalebone with pierced and carved decoration and ivory ring. Length: 2 inches.

Fig. 75
Tin rattle, U.S., late nineteenth century. Boy's head of molded tin painted black. Possibly made for an African-American child. Wooden handle with whistle tip. Length: 6 inches. From the collection of Ada Ghiron Segal.

styles like the molded boy's head rattle shown here were also made (Fig. 74 and 75).

These toys were very inexpensive, and a newspaper advertisement of the period offered wholesale prices of $2 per dozen for unpainted tin rattles and $6 per dozen for painted ones. A little later in the century, wood rattles sold for 17¢ to 37¢ per dozen, and Indian rubber rattles for $1.75 per dozen!

As manufacturing methods improved, more elaborate forms of tin rattles were made. A modified version of coral-and-bells rattle in painted tin with a wood handle and a whistle was a much enjoyed children's party favor in the late nineteenth and early twentieth century (Fig. 76 and 77). Many handsome toys of painted tin continued to be made in the United States and Europe until World War II, but beautiful and rare examples of trains, fire engines, and airplanes were lost because children were encouraged to donate their metal toys to the war effort in the 1940s.

Parallel to the expanding variety of manufactured toys, including rattles, handmade and homemade pieces continued to be produced. After the Civil War, in the newly poor South, tin snuffboxes were covered with bright-colored crochet yarn and strung together to make baby rattles; pebbles inside the box provided the noisemakers. Displaced Confederate Army soldiers, working their way westward in the 1870s and after, became casual farm laborers on their way. To help earn their keep, they whittled or carved objects of scrap wood. Boxes, letter-holders, and even pieces of furniture were fashioned into intricately interlocked

constructions, often with distinctive sawtooth edging. Baby rattles were also among the items made (Fig. 78, 79, and 80). The general term for this type of woodworking is "tramp art" and it is in great demand by collectors today. Tramp art continued to be made until after World War I, demonstrating again how folk art flourishes in the face of privation.

Wood, straw, and cloth were fashioned into rattles and teethers, of course, during all of America's history. One of the styles that became a favorite in the latter half of the nineteenth century was the "whimsy," a triumph of the whittler's art. Carved from one piece of wood, a variety of forms evolved. A simple rod with rings sliding on it was one kind (Fig. 81). A hollow carved frame with the wood ball visible inside was another type (Fig. 82), and other styles existed too, only limited by the imagination and virtuosity of the maker (Fig. 83).

Stuffed cloth rattles and dolls with pebbles or similar material inside or bells attached outside were other popular homemade toys in the latter-nineteenth century. Mounted on a stick, they made for a simple but enjoyable plaything (Fig. 84). Rattles made of strips of leather forming a loose frame, with tin or brass bells fastened to the strips, and with a wood handle, were also in common use, as were rattles made of a single rod of wood with bells attached (Fig. 85). Some are still made today in rural areas.

By the late nineteenth century the United States had become a fully industrialized country. Many objects which were formerly luxuries were now machine-made and affordable by a larger propor-

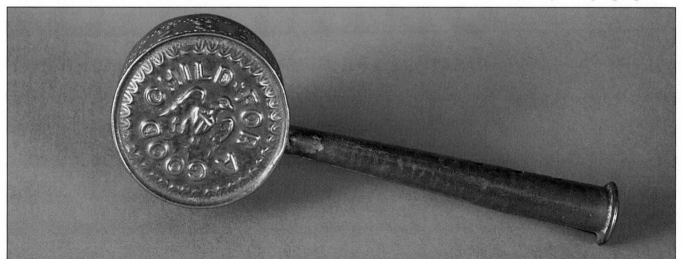

Fig. 74
Tin rattle, U.S., c.1880-1890. Drum-shaped rattle stamped "For A Good Child." Has a tin handle with a whistle and holes so it may be played as a fife. Length: 5-1/2 inches.

Fig. 76
Postcard photograph, U.S., c.1910. The baby is holding a tin rattle with bells. See Fig. 77.

Fig. 77
Painted tin rattle, U.S., c.1910. Multicolor stripes on ball-shaped body. It has tin bells and a wooden handle with a whistle tip. Length: 6 inches.

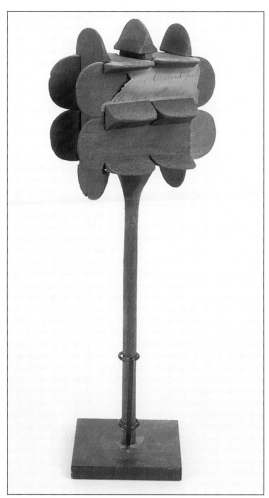

Fig. 78
Tramp art rattle, U.S., c.1860s. This rattle has intricate interlocking small wooden laths, which rattle when shaken. Believed to be a Civil War prisoner's work. Length: 6-1/2 inches.

Fig. 80
Tramp art rattle, U.S., c.1870. Interlocking pieces of dark-stained wood with saw-tooth edging. Length: 7 inches.

Fig. 79
Tramp art rattle, U.S., mid-nineteenth century. As in Fig. 78, interlocking pieces of wood are combined with small interlocking wooden laths. Carved wooden handle is inscribed "Blanche 1856" on handle. Length: 5-1/2 inches.

Fig. 81
Whimsy rattle, U.S., early twentieth century. Center rod and sliding rings carved from one piece of dark-stained wood. Length: 8 inches.

Fig. 82
Whimsy rattle, U.S., c.1890. Openwork carved wooden rattle with wooden ball visible inside. Length: 5-3/4 inches.

Fig. 83
Folk Art rattle, U.S., early twentieth century. Unusually shaped wooden rattle with retractable bobbles, wooden handle. Length: 6-1/2 inches.

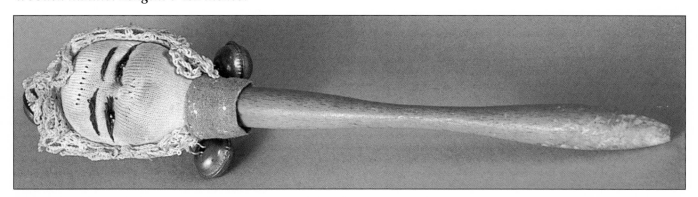

Fig. 84
Cloth rattle, U.S., early twentieth century. Stuffed doll head with painted face and calico– and lace-trimmed bonnet. Two bells are attached to the head, and it is on a wooden stick. Length: 9 inches.

Fig. 85
Folk Art rattle, U.S., c.1930s. Version of an earlier style usually made in leather. Has brass bells and a painted wooden handle. Length: 7 inches.

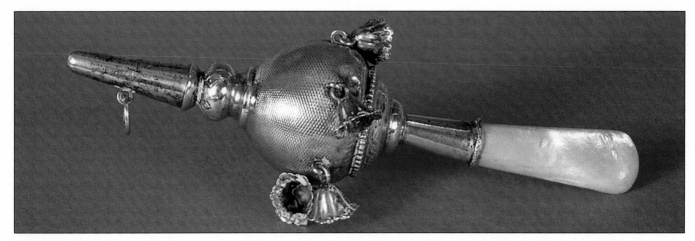

Fig. 86
Silver rattle, U.S., 1870-1890. Finely engraved design on silver bulb-shaped body. Has silver bells and a mother-of-pearl handle. Marked "Sterling."Length: 5 inches.

Fig. 87
Cat rattle, U.S., c.1910-1915. Silver with ivory handle and two silver bells. Has a realistic cat's head emerging from barrel. Marked "Sterling."Length: 3-1/2 inches.

tion of the population. Silver and silver plate could now be made into articles originally made by hand. But these were not the only changes, for the public's tastes were changing too. Prosperity in urban centers gave citizens disposable income. Decoration and furniture became elaborate and fussy, and the "Gilded Age," as the period was known, came to be a symbol for the excesses of the newly rich and the people who copied their extravagant displays.

Baby rattles and teethers of the period followed suit. Ivory and mother-of-pearl handles on silver rattles took the place of earlier tin and wicker models, and the designs began to reflect the figures in popular culture and entertainment for children. Echoes of heavily decorated late Victorian English rattles were still to be found in rattles, but

evidences of purely American style began to develop (Fig. 86).

Silver was inexpensive, and rattles with a great variety of motifs were made, chiefly by manufacturers of table silver. Cats, rabbits, and dogs were favorite themes for rattles, along with flowers, hearts, and angels (Fig. 87). Santa Claus was one of the first characters used in rattles, and Mother Goose and Nursery Rhyme scenes appeared as well (Fig. 88). Teething rings of ivory or mother-of-pearl, hung with silver bells, were a common shape at the beginning of the twentieth century. One company made them with the baby's birthstone imbedded in the ivory ring. These are exceedingly rare today. A silver handle, identical to the manufacturer's flatware pattern, was sometimes added to the ring with bells (Fig. 89). The silverware

Fig. 89
Teething ring rattle. c.1910-1920. Mother-of-pearl ring with two silver bells attached, mounted on a silver cutlery handle. Marked "Sterling."Length: 5 inches.

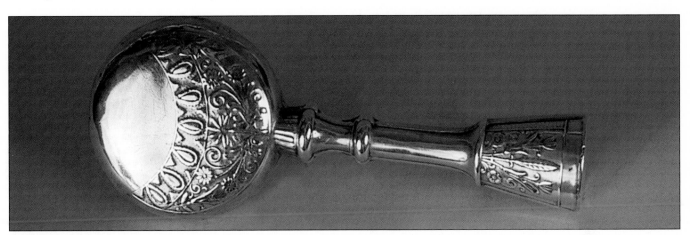

Fig. 90
Watch case rattle, U.S., early twentieth century. Replica of a watch case with floral embossing and pierced-work decoration. Silver handle, marked "Gorham Sterling"on stem. Diameter: 1-1/2 inches; overall length: 5-1/2 inches.

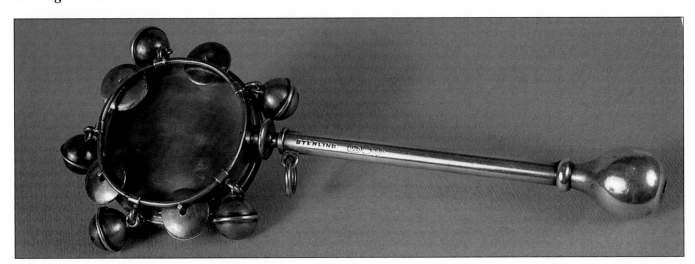

Fig. 91
Tambourine rattle, U.S., 1886. Silver with five bells and silver handle with a whistle tip. Engraved "To Reggie from Mammelie, 1886."Marked "Sterling"on handle. Length 5 3/4 inches.

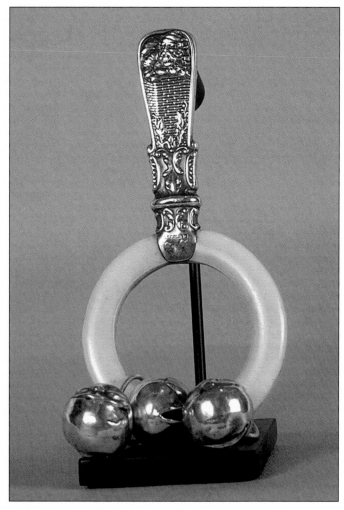

Fig. 88
Santa Claus rattle, U.S., c.1910. Santa is descending the chimney on the silver handle which is riveted to an ivory ring. The bells attached to the ring have Santa Claus faces. Marked "Sterling."Length: 4 inches.

designer's ingenuity produced rattles made of watch cases or miniatures of musical instruments (Fig. 90 and 91).

Around the turn of the century in both Britain and the United States the "stub" handle for baby rattles seemed to become the one with the most appeal. This was a broad, thick handle of mother-of-pearl, supporting a pressed silver capital in a wide range of designs, with two silver bells attached—a variation of the clapper-style rattle. The thick handle was easy for the baby to grasp and safe to put in its mouth (Fig. 92 and 93). Simpler teethers in ivory and mother-of-pearl are characteristic of the era as well (Fig. 94, 95, and 96).

As a reaction against the overblown decoration in clothing, furniture, and architecture at the end of the nineteenth century, new attitudes arose in the art field. Stylized natural forms, based on nature and human curves, became the design elements of the style known as "Art Nouveau." The style strongly influenced the paintings and home furnishings of the period between 1890 and World War I. Art Nouveau was widely adopted in Europe. In France and England it flourished in the graphic arts and architecture, as well as jewelry and house-hold objects, and of course rattles (Fig. 97, 98, 99, and 100).

Soon after the turn of the twentieth century, cartoon figures began to appear in baby rattles in the United States. These were among the first representations of an original American cultural icon. Buster Brown and his dog, Tige, had great appeal for children (Fig. 101). The Kewpie doll, first illustrated by Rose O'Neill in 1912, was such a successful little creature that it was made into dolls,

Fig. 92
Stub rattle, U.S., early twentieth century. Silver baby's head in elaborate bonnet that has two bells attached, with a thick mother-of-pearl stub handle. Marked "Sterling."Length: 5 inches.

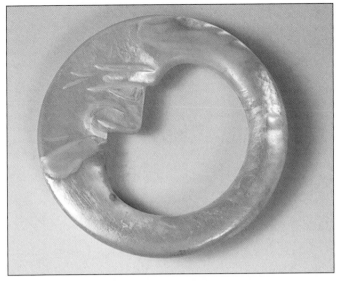

Fig. 93
Two stub rattles, U.S., early twentieth century.
Left: lollipop-shaped rattle with man-in-the-moon
face. Its mother-of-pearl stub handle may have
been ground down. Stamped "William S. Scher-
ber."Length: 2-3/4 inches; right: silver rattle with
two bells showing chick emerging from egg; has a
mother-of-pearl stub handle. Length: 3-1/2 inches.

Fig. 95
Mother-of-pearl teether, U.S., c.1915-1920. Carved
man-in-the-moon face on a mother-of-pearl ring.
Diameter: 2-1/2 inches.

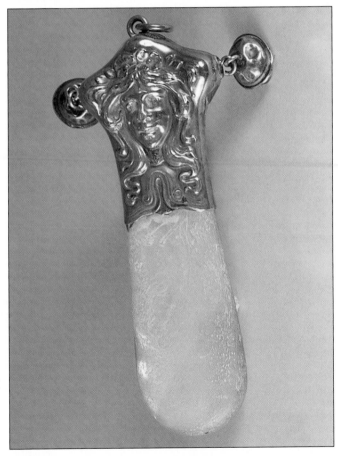

Fig. 94
Teether, U.S., c.1910. Patinated ivory of the man-
in-the-moon's profile. Length 3-3/4 inches.

Fig. 98
Art Nouveau rattle, U.S., c.1900-1910. Silver rattle
with long-haired woman and flower motifs characteristic of Art Nouveau style. It has two silver
bells and a mother-of-pearl handle. Marked "Sterling."Length: 5 inches. From the collection of Ada
Ghiron Segal.

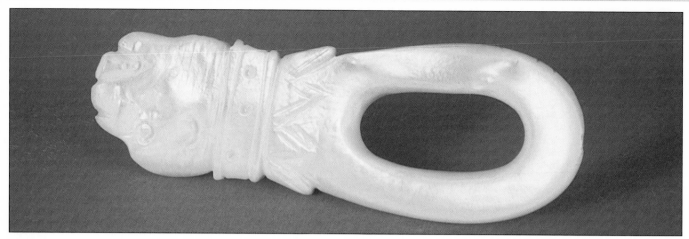

Fig. 96
Teether, U.S., c.1920-1930. Mother-of-pearl carved in shape of baby's hand at one end and a loop opening as a handle at the other end. Length: 3-1/2 inches.

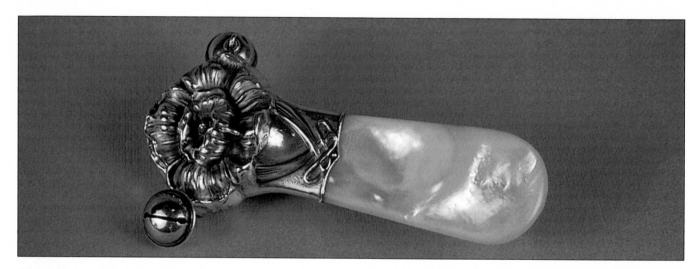

Fig. 97
Art Nouveau rattle, U.S., c.1900. Stub-handle rattle with a silver top with floral design in high relief and two silver bells. Marked "Sterling." Length 3-1/4 inches.

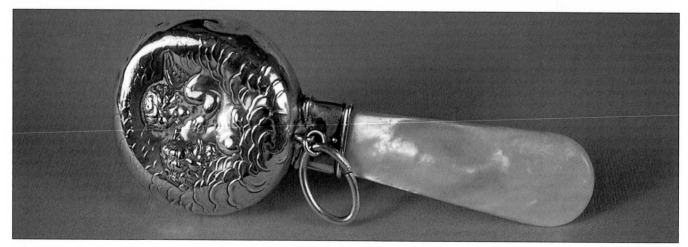

Fig. 99
Art Nouveau rattle, U.S., c.1900-1910. Mother holding baby shown in high relief. The curving lines are typical of this art style. Silver with mother-of-pearl handle. Made by Unger Brothers of Newark, New Jersey. Length: 4 inches.

Fig. 101
Buster Brown rattle, U.S., c.1915. Depiction of a popular comic character. Embossed "Buster" on the front with the small boy; the dog, Tige, is pictured on the back of the rattle with "Tige" embossed below. Ivory ring. Marked "Sterling." Length 1-1/4 inches.

Fig. 102
Kewpie Doll rattle, U.S., c.1915-1920. The little figure with the topknot was a favorite subject for toys, dolls, and household articles. The rattle is molded silver with an ivory ring. Length 1-3/4 inches.

Fig. 100
Jester rattle, U.S., c.1900-1910. Art Nouveau interpretation of the classic jester, with elongated body hung with silver bells. The ring, which was probably mother-of-pearl, is missing. Marked "Gorham Sterling." Length: 4 inches. From the collection Ada Ghiron Segal.

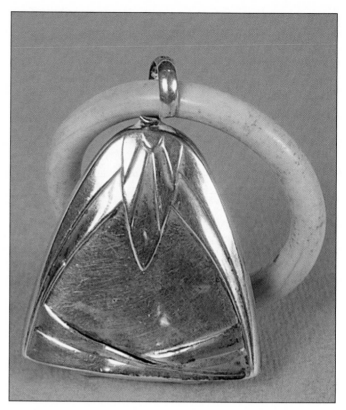

Fig. 104
Art Deco rattle, U.S., 1930. Silver bell with geometric Art Deco styling; has an ivory ring. Marked "Sterling." Length: 1-1/2 inches.

Fig. 103
Minstrel Man rattle, U.S., c.1915-1920. Brightly colored celluloid figure of a popular entertainment character. Height: 6-1/2 inches. From the collection of Ada Ghiron Segal.

Fig. 105
Art Deco rattle, U.S., c.1930s. Stylized dachshund motif—the breed was popular at the time. Embossed silver with ivory ring. Marked "Sterling." Diameter: 1-1/2 inches.

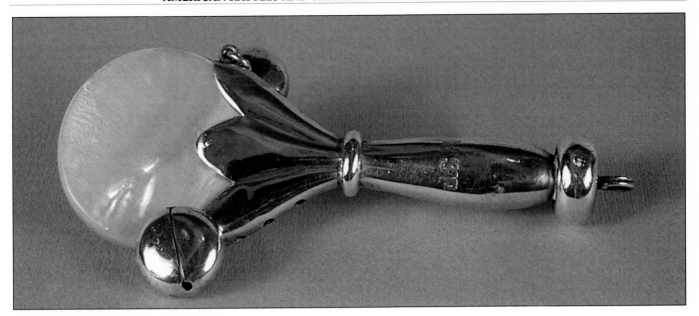

Fig. 106
Art Deco rattle, U.S., c.1925. Thick mother-of-pearl disc mounted in heavy silver with two silver bells. Marked "Tiffany." Length: 4-1/2 inches.

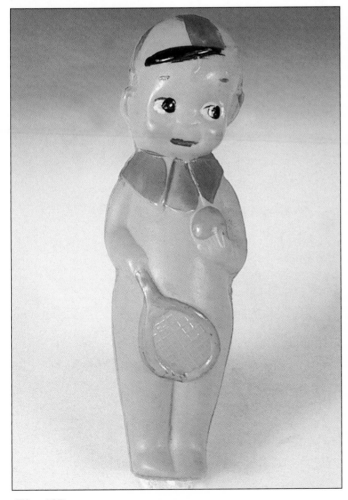

Fig. 107
Celluloid rattle, U.S., 1930s. Little girl in sports attire holding tennis racquet. Traces of bright color remain. Height: 3 inches.

Fig. 108
Bowling Pin rattle, U.S., c.1935. Silver bowling pin rattle with engraved monogram in front. The loop is missing its ring or ribbon. Marked "Sterling." Length: 3-1/2 inches.

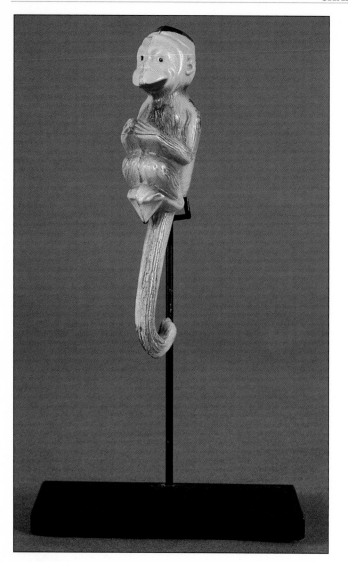

Fig. 109
French Telephone rattle, U.S., c.1935. Silver dumbbell-style, shaped like a French telephone. Marked "Sterling" and "Webster." Length: 3-1/2 inches.

Fig. 111
Celluloid rattle, U.S., 1930s. Painted monkey, holding a bunch of bananas, has a long tail forming handle. Length: 4-1/2 inches.

Fig. 115
Humpty-Dumpty rattle, U.S., c.1940. Painted celluloid egghead; body and legs are of Bakelite beads. Length 4-1/2 inches.

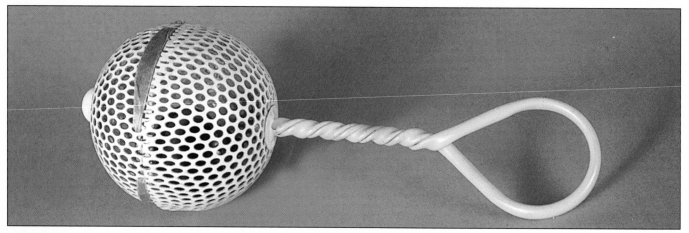

Fig. 110
Celluloid rattle, U.S., 1930s. Pierced work ball-shape designed which looks like ivory. Brass bell or bead is visible inside. Length: 5 inches.

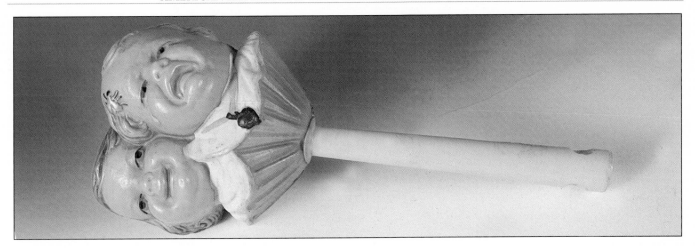

Fig. 112
Celluloid rattle, U.S., 1930s. This colorful molded celluloid shows smiling and crying baby faces. Length: 6-1/4 inches.

Fig. 113
Celluloid rattle, U.S., 1930s. Native American boy and girl are shown paddling a canoe. Length: 5-1/4 inches.

Fig. 114
Bakelite rattle, U.S., c.1940. Ocean liner with black smokestack. Length: 6 inches.

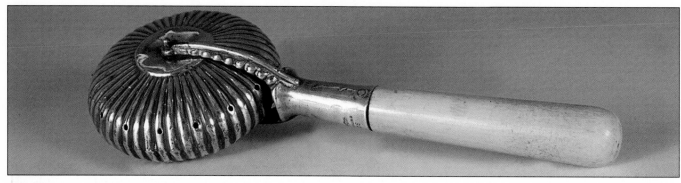

Fig. 116
Spinner rattle, U.S., 1950s. Silver twirling wheel with striated incising pattern. Silver with silver handles; the noisemakers are inside the wheel. Marked "Sterling."Length: 6 inches.

Fig. 117
Twist-handle rattle, U.S., 1950s. Silver rattle in cruciform shape with two large bells and whistle top. Heart-shaped center plaque is engraved "Baby."Marked "Sterling."Length: 5 inches.

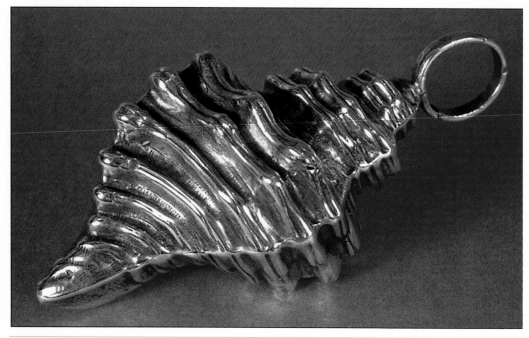

Fig. 118
Conch Shell rattle, U.S., 1950s. Heavy silver in realistic shell form. The ring is missing. Marked "Sterling."Length: 4-1/2 inches.

household objects, and rattles for many years. There is a brisk market today for Kewpie doll items (Fig. 102). Other well-known characters also appeared in rattles, like the cheerful minstrel man, a popular entertainment figure of the time (Fig. 103).

Following the turmoil of World War I there was a worldwide desire for simplicity and the shedding of the past. Groups of artists in Germany, France, and England began to envision a new art form—streamlined, with restrained geometric decoration. They made furniture, textiles, clothing, jewelry, and household objects with sleek, clean lines and minimal decorative details. This style, called "Art Deco" remained a major movement in the 1920s and '30s and paved the way for the Modern Art styles that came after World War II (Fig. 104, 105, and 106).

Other developments coincided in time with these artistic changes. More leisure time led to many new interests. Sports became part of middle-class life and pastimes like tennis and golf were pursued. Baby rattles soon reflected these new activities of a child's parents (Fig. 107). Even bowling as a pastime was translated into baby rattle form (Fig. 108). When the French-style telephone was invented in the early 1930s, sure enough, a baby rattle in that form rapidly appeared (Fig. 109)! Newer cartoon figures like Popeye and Mickey and Minnie Mouse soon replaced old favorites as baby rattle motifs (Fig. 43).

During the 1930s and '40s, new synthetic materials took precedence over some of the traditional ones. Tin rattles, for example, disappeared, and

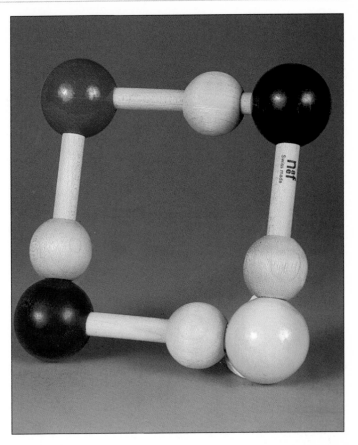

Fig. 119
Educational toy rattle, U.S., 1980s. Natural wooden frame with painted wooden balls that click together when shaken. Width: 3-1/2 inches.

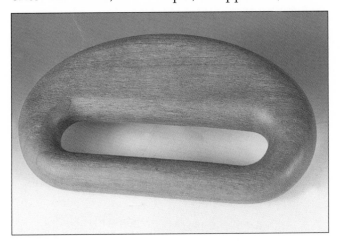

Fig. 121
Artisan's rattle, U.S., 1980s. Natural wood carved into an easy-to-hold shape. Has pebbles inside. Arkansas craftsman's creation. Width: 3 inches.

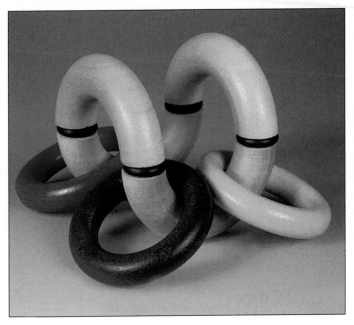

Fig. 120
Educational toy rattle, U.S., 1980s. Bentwood frame of natural wood with brightly painted rings; a modern variation of the beads-on-a-string rattle form. Width: 3-1/2 inches.

celluloid toys and dolls, although still made in vast numbers, were being supplanted. Most of the celluloid toys had been made in Japan, which unlike today, then had a reputation for inexpensive manufactured goods (Fig. 110, 111, 112, and 113). Bakelite and similar resins were used for baby rattles and teethers, but were less desirable. Although they were less fragile than celluloid, Bakelite rattles and toys could not be made in the really bright colors children love (Fig. 114 and 115).

Although clowns, animals, and doll motifs continued to be used for baby rattles, new forms in furniture and textiles in the 1950s had their influence on baby rattles. Rounded and organic shapes were introduced in the decorative arts, and there was a striving for new expressions in the interpre-

tation of "modern" design. Some silver rattles give an indication of the lack of direction, or perhaps lack of a unified artistic vision, that had motivated the craftsmen of the past (Fig. 116, 117, and 118).

In the 1970s, a backlash against the world of artificial things seemed to capture the imagination of a generation of young people. Natural foods and natural materials were sought out, and in some cases, reinvented, as in a return to organic farming methods. As a corollary to this, there was a desire for toys made of wood instead of plastics. Having children experience the tactile qualities of natural wood was thought to be an aid to their development. In answer to this demand, progressive toy manufacturers worked with educators to produce wood toys conforming to these ideas. Baby rattles

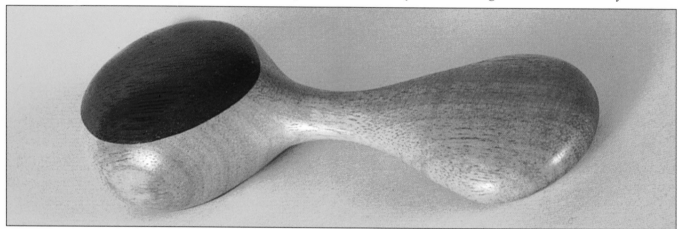

Fig. 122
Artisan's rattle, U.S., 1980s. Lollipop shape in two tones of natural wood. Made by an Oregon craftsman. Length: 3-1/2 inches.

Fig. 123
Artisan's rattle, U.S., 1990s. Two tones of wood in the shape of a Good Humor ice-cream bar on a stick. Made by Robert McHenry Zoll, Wurtsboro, New York. Length: 6 inches.

were included among these toys; some of the designs went back to century-old prototypes of the clapper and the sistrum (Fig. 119 and 120).

The recent revival of interest in American crafts has again brought individually-made toys to the public's attention. Rattles, which are beautifully finished and are a pleasure for a baby to handle, are currently being made by young craftsmen. Usually they are carved in fine woods and are not very expensive (Fig. 121, 122, and 123).

But most of today's baby rattles and teethers are made of plastics of various types. They have smooth, rounded edges to protect the child from injury and are colored with non-toxic paints. Most of them are imported from China and Taiwan, and mass-production and shoddy materials have taken away their individuality and charm. These plastic rattles have the advantage of being inexpensive and easy to clean. Few survive being tossed about by an active child and they are usually just thrown away when they are broken. They sell for a dollar or two and are no great loss to the world when they are discarded. However, they do tell us a lot about the current icons that appeal to children. Miss Piggy and Snoopy may very well be the collectibles of the future, if they are not already (Fig. 124 and 125).

Silver rattles as gifts for births and christenings are still being sold today in jewelry stores and baby shops across the United States. Bells and dumbbells

are the leading choices, but bears, rabbits, and lions are also available. Silver teething rings have come again into the market, after a long absence. Occasionally, an art museum shop or an exclusive jeweler will offer a reproduction of an antique rattle in its Christmas catalogue. Sterling silver rattles and teethers of today are still relatively expensive and range in price from $40 to $100.

While it is probably true that most children throughout the western hemisphere today are given plastic rattles, there are still homemade and folk art rattles made by the loving hands of a parent or craftsman. The ornate and precious baby rattles and teethers of bygone days have vanished. But babies still love rattles. The sound, movement,

Fig. 124
Miss Piggy rattle, U.S., 1990s. Blow-up plastic doll of popular television character. The rattle is weighted at the bottom with sand or pebbles. Height: 9-1/2 inches.

Fig. 125
Snoopy rattle, U.S., 1990s. Reclining Snoopy atop a bi-colored plastic ball rattle. Diameter: 3-1/2 inches.

Fig. 127
Oil Painting, England, 1757.
Portrait of a young girl holding
a very large gold coral-and-
bells. Unsigned, but dated on
the back. Height: 30 inches;
Width: 25 inches.

British Rattles: Royalty and Nursery Rhymes

"Look, look what's here! A dainty golden thing!
See how the dancing bells turn round, and ring
To please my bantling."

Francis Quarles (1592-1644)

As we have seen, the superstition that coral contained magic, protective, and curative powers has its roots in antiquity. This belief endured for hundreds of years and coexisted with the use of rattles and teethers to amuse and comfort children. The combination of coral with a rattle or teething stick arose in the Mediterranean area and spread throughout Europe. But it was in Great Britain that the coral-and-bells rattle had its finest flowering.

Very few records remain of the life of children in the British Isles before the Norman Conquest in 1066 A.D. We may assume, however, that some sort of rattle existed, because there are references in medieval documents to the use of a coral amulet to avert "fascination," the name used at the time for the evil eye cast upon children.

Before the coral-and bells came into common use in Britain, though, simple silver bow-shaped rattles with bells attached by chains and a bit of coral imbedded in the center of the bow were used. They were derivative of the seahorse and mermaid types of Mediterranean rattles. These rattles were prevalent until the beginning of the sixteenth century when the coral-and-bells took their place.

Although England was not the first country to adopt the coral-and-bells type of rattle, that style has become most closely identified with it. Coral-and-bells rattles had been in use in Italy since the Renaissance period. However, this trinket seems to have captured the hearts of the British, and the style prevailed for several centuries.

The coral-and-bells, also called baby-bells, whistles, or coral-sticks in Britain, seems to have been a necessary accoutrement of wealth and status. This is attested to by the many references to the coral-and-bells in English literature. As early as 1600, Beaumont and Fletcher mentioned "coral wissels" in a play. Among other writers, Alexander Pope, Thomas Hood, and Thomas Carlyle referred to coral-and-bells in their writings. Coral-and-bells were common enough among the aristocracy to be satirized in print. Political cartoons in the last days of George III mocked his senility by showing him with a rattle, and Thomas Hood criticized the extravagance of coral-and-bells by writing "Baby cutting her first little toothy-peg with a fifty guinea rattle."

Conquest and trade bought great wealth to England starting with the Elizabethan period, and the arts flourished. Paintings of children, beginning with the royal offspring, became widespread

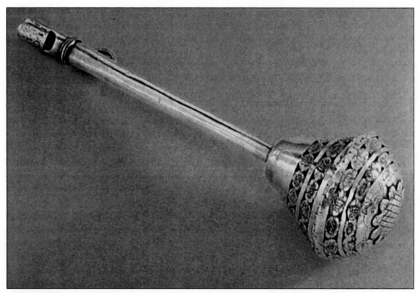

Fig. 126
Pierced-work rattle, England, c.1620. Silver with silver handle and floral decoration. Marked MC/HL. Length: 6-1/2 inches. Exhibition Catalogue, Save the Children, 1982.

Fig. 128
Watercolor painting, Scotland, c.1830. The sitter, Elizabeth Fraser Beveridge Duncan, is holding a small coral-and-bells. The off-shoulder dress was a big fashion for little girls at the time. 4-1/2 inches wide by 3-1/2 inches high.

among the aristocracy. One of the earliest depictions of a child with a rattle is the portrait of Edward IV, son of Henry VIII (See Fig. 8). The little boy is holding a gold rattle in a bulb shape, decorated with pierce-work and delicate engraving. The handle, which may be coral or gold, cannot be seen clearly. A silver rattle pictured here, which is similar in style and with a silver handle, is dated c.1600 (Fig. 126). A portrait of Elizabeth, daughter of James I, painted about 1589 shows the little girl holding a large gold coral-and-bells attached to her waist by a ribbon, and the British Museum has an engraving dated 1587 in which a coral-and-bells is easily recognizable. The portrait of an elaborately dressed little girl shown here is unsigned, but dated 1757 on the back (Fig. 127). She is holding a very large gold coral-and-bells fastened by a ribbon

to her waist. The rattle was probably too heavy for her to carry.

Miniature portraits on ivory and vellum were painted in England as early as the latter half of the fifteenth century. Many of these were of children, some of whom were holding rattles. The techniques of miniature painting came to England through the early illustrated manuscripts of Flanders, Ghent, and Bruges. Miniature paintings of royal princes and princesses were exchanged throughout Europe to help arrange royal marriages. In later times, portraits of children and sweethearts were given as keepsakes to fathers and husbands away at war or establishing Britain's far-flung colonies. Miniature paintings remained in fashion until photographs took their place in the mid-nineteenth century (Fig. 128 and 129).

Fig. 129
Oil Painting, England, c.1835-1840. The little girl is holding a woven straw rattle on a ribbon.
Artist unknown. Height: 7 inches; Width: 6 inches.

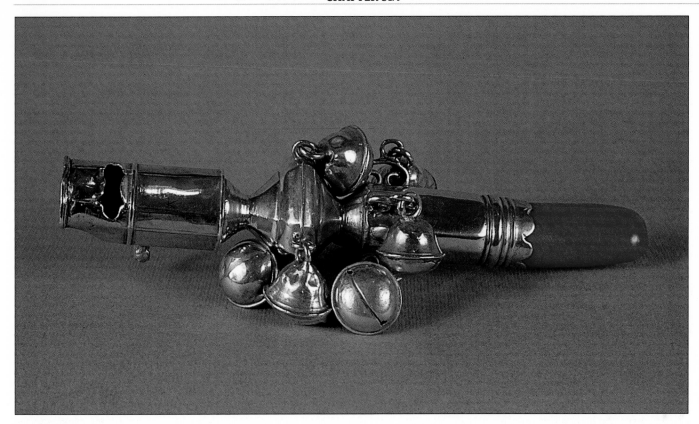

Fig. 130
Coral-and-bells rattle, England, George I, c.1720. Silver, stem in octagonal shape, with original bells and a thick coral handle. No marks. Length: 5-1/2 inches.

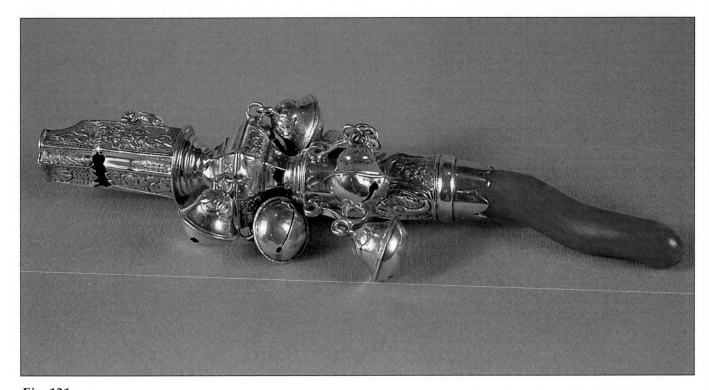

Fig. 131
Coral-and-bells rattle, England, George II, c.1735. Silver, with original bells; has a whistle tip and thick coral handle, as well as delicate brightwork decoration. Hallmark: "W.T." (William Tookey). Length: 6-1/2 inches.

Fig. 132
Coral-and-bells rattle, England, 1807. Regency style in two tones of vermeil. Has its original bells, a whistle tip, and a coral handle. No maker's mark. Length: 5-1/2 inches.

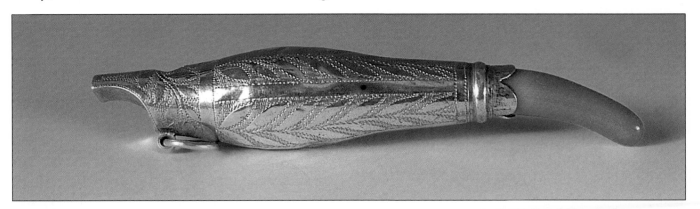

Fig. 133
Coral and Vermeil teether, England, c.1810. Geometric brightwork design, whistle tip, and a thick coral handle. No maker's mark. Length: 3-1/2 inches.

Fig. 134
Coral-and-bells rattle, England, c.1745. Silver with eight original bells and a whistle tip. Ivory handle is painted to look like coral. Initials "R.C." engraved on whistle. Attributed to Sandyland Drinkwater, London. Length: 5-1/2 inches.

The eighteenth century marked the start of the great period in English art. The golden age of painting, furniture, decoration, and metalwork is considered to be the period from George I in 1711 through George III in 1793. The beautifully wrought objects of the Georgian period are thought to be among the finest ever made.

Georgian period design is characterized by a Neo-Classic sense of elegance and proportion, with restrained decorative details. Luxury items like silver platters, serving pieces, teapots, and bowls followed these precepts. Baby rattles, extremely popular at the time, also expressed these design elements.

At the beginning of the Georgian period, coral-and-bells rattles had modified octagonal shapes called "eight-squares." These were made of fairly heavy silver and had thick coral handles. As a general rule, the thicker the coral, the older the piece (Fig. 130 and 131). The whistle tip became an integral part of the rattle, and gold, silver, and vermeil were used for the body of the rattle and the bells (Fig. 132). A little further into the 1700s, more bulbous shapes evolved. Teethers with coral sticks were very similar to the rattles in style, but they lacked bells (Fig. 133).

At this time England became famous for the extraordinary skill of its gold and silversmiths. The craftsmen who made spoons, snuffboxes, sugar tongs, and baby rattles were called "smallworkers." Antique dealers today still refer to items like these as "silver smalls." London, Dublin, and Edinburgh were the chief centers for silverwork, but Birmingham soon became noted for its smallworkers. By the 1770s, gold and silversmiths were organized into guilds and their work was identified with individual marks that identified the place, year, and maker. Birmingham, for example, is always indicated by a small anchor. Some craftsmen were not admitted into the guilds or could not afford to join, so there are many authentic Georgian and Victorian pieces without marks. Many of the very old pieces have had their hallmarks worn away, so the collector can only be guided by stylistic details.

Many of the Georgian silversmiths became very well known for their work. Among these were John Richardson, John Shaw, T.S. Matthews, and Sandyland Drinkwater. They gained a reputation for excellence which has lasted for more than two hundred years (Fig. 134).

Women became silversmiths, too. It was not uncommon for a widow or daughter to take over the family business when the head of the family died. Eliza Tookey (Fig. 135), Alice Sheen, and Louisa Courtauld are among those whose work is known, but the most famous of the women silversmiths is Hester Bateman (Fig. 136). After the death of her husband in 1761, she entered her own mark at the Goldsmith's Hall and went about expanding her husband's smallwork firm with the help of her sons and daughter-in-law. By using sheet-rolled

Fig. 135
Coral-and-bells rattle, England, 1773. Vermeil in baluster shape, geometric brightwork, with six original bells and a whistle tip. Hallmark: Eliza Tookey, London. Length: 4-3/4 inches.

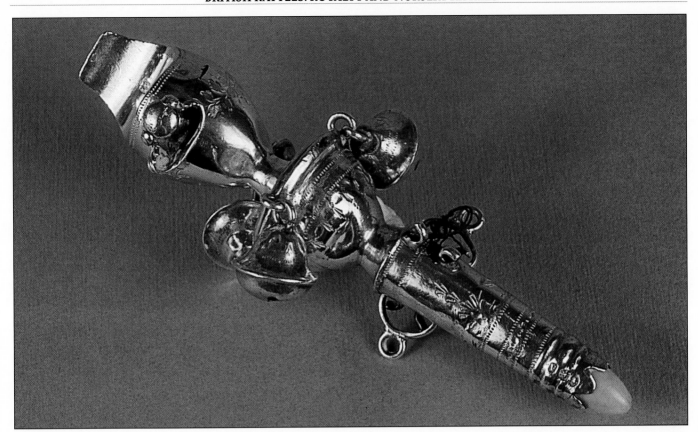

Fig. 136
Coral-and-bells rattle, England, 1793. Silver rattle in modified baluster shape, with four original bells and a whistle tip. Second tier of bells is missing. This unusual white coral handle may have been a replacement. Hallmark: Peter, Ann, and Hester Bateman. Length: 4-7/8 inches.

Fig. 137
Coral-and-bells rattle, England, 1810. Tri-color gold rattle with exceptionally fine brightwork, gold bells, whistle tip, and a thick coral handle. Hallmark: Ray and Montague. Length: 4-7/8 inches. Courtesy S.J. Shrubsole Corp., Ney York City.

Fig. 138
Coral-and-bells rattle, England, 1861. Silver with whistle tip; some bells are missing. Has ornate scroll decoration and a thin coral stick. Hallmark: "G.U." for George Unita. Length: 4-1/2 inches.

Fig. 139
Coral-and-bells rattle, England, 1869. Elaborate silver with a whistle tip and decorated bells. Coral may have been replaced because it does not fit perfectly into holder. Hallmark: "G.U." for George Unita. Length: 5-1/2 inches.

Fig. 140
Coral-and-bells rattle, England, 1880. Silver with heavy late Victorian embellished design. Has its five original bells and a whistle tip. Coral stick has been repaired with a silver band, but it appears to be the original piece. Hallmark: "G.U." for George Unita. Length: 5-7/8 inches.

silver and pressed decoration to replace the traditional methods of hand-raising, engraving, and casting, she was able to achieve an enormous output.

Although electroplating has been around since Roman times, it was not commercially applied until the early 1800s. As a growing number of machine-stamped and pressed articles came into being, baby rattles among them, silver plate was often used for small items. The strict rules of British law insisted that they be marked as plate. Collectors can look for the initials "EPNS" to indicate that the table silver or rattle is Electro-Plated Nickel Silver. Not every piece of silver plate is marked this way in modern times, and often only testing will determine if the object is sterling or silver-plated. Dealers have a simple test to prove the article is sterling.

By the Regency period, from 1793 to 1832 when Victoria became Queen of England, English design had become more decorative and had begun to absorb rococo elements (Fig. 137). Early Victorian style followed this same trend, and the prosperity of England and the wealth of the expanding middle class led to more and more elaborate styles. Details of furniture, architecture, and clothing became complicated and overly ornamented.

The progress of this sort of decoration can also be seen in the baby rattles and teethers of the period. Rattles became more ornate and the coral sticks became thinner. The epitome of the progression of this style in rattles can be seen in the later work of George Unita, a famous London silver-smith who produced rattles until the 1880s. They are heavy with overblown decoration, the function of this simple toy almost being lost in order to increase the prestige of the child's family (Fig. 138, 139, and 140).

England was the world's leading power during the mid- to late-Victorian era, and trade with its colonies soon brought new materials to the market. Gradually ivory and mother-of-pearl began to replace coral as handles for baby rattles. Although coral-and-bells continues to be made by individual silversmiths, by the mid-1870s the taste for this type of rattle had passed. The belief in coral for its curative and protective powers faded away in the light of new scientific and medical discoveries (Fig. 141 and 142). Ivory and mother-of-pearl teethers supplanted the silver and coral ones (Fig. 143 and 144). In the late nineteenth and early twentieth centuries, celluloid and tin rattles were made in Britain, but the silver ones remained the popular choice.

Around the turn of the twentieth century the most common form became known as the "stub" rattle. This was a silver or silver-plated top with a stamped or pressed motif with two bells attached, mounted on a broad, thick piece of mother-of-pearl. These rattles are not too difficult to find today at antique shows and flea markets (Fig. 145, 146, and 147).

The spread of literacy and leisure gave rise to new interests in Britain at the end of the nineteenth century. Elements of popular culture and the development of a body of literature for children intro-

Fig. 141
Owl rattle, England, late nineteenth century. The owl represents the gift of wisdom wished for the baby. Pressed design in silver with two bells; the ring is missing. Thin coral handle. Birmingham mark. Height: 3 inches.

duced new subjects to be portrayed in baby rattles. Kate Greenaway, an author and illustrator of children's books in the 1880s, had her little girl heroines portrayed in rattles and teethers (Fig. 148). Punch and Judy puppet shows, distant cousins of the Italian *Commedia del l'Arte*, had entertained British children for generations. Punch or a jester-figure was often used as a motif for rattles (Fig. 149, 150, and 151). Mother Goose and fairytale characters were also very popular. The teddy bear, based on the cuddly Australian koala bear, was a beloved object that soon appeared on rattles, as did dogs, cats, rabbits, monkeys, and other animals (Fig. 152).

Toward the end of the nineteenth century, other characters from children's books and popular culture appeared on rattles, including Lewis Carroll's Alice, March Hare, White Rabbit, and Dormouse (Fig. 153). In *Through the Looking Glass*

Carroll even wrote "Tweedledum and Twee-dledee/Agreed to have a battle/For Tweedledum said Tweedledee/Had spoiled his nice new rattle." The Golliwog, a puppet boy whose adventures were loosely based on native life in British colonies, was created in books by Bertha Upton in 1910. The character was so popular that a cakewalk was named after it, and a Golliwog rattle soon followed (Fig. 154). And, when the Boy Scouts were established in 1912, by General Baden-Powell, a Boy Scout rattle appeared soon afterward (Fig. 155).

Queen Mary, the wife of George V, began her reign in 1903. She set the style in many areas of fashion and decoration. She was particularly fond of dolls and amassed a large collection of them. She commissioned an elaborate doll house, complete in every detail, including a baby layette and rattles. The doll house was the envy of every little British girl, and was widely copied in simpler forms. Doll

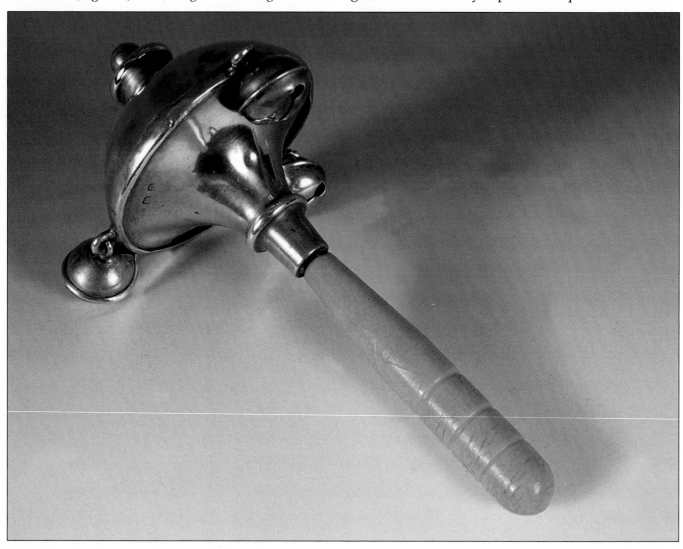

Fig. 142
Umbrella rattle, England, 1896. Silver with original bells and an ivory handle. Hallmarked with lion for London. Length: 4-1/2 inches.

Fig. 143
Ivory teether,
England, late
nineteenth
century. Carved
jester face in
profile. Fixed balls
once held blue
ribbons and small
ivory beads.
Length: 4-1/2
inches.

Fig. 145
Nursery Rhyme
rattle, England,
c.1900. Silver with
two replaced bells,
a stub mother-of-
pearl handle, and a
whistle tip. Pressed
design of "The Cat
and the Fiddle."
Birmingham mark.
Length: 3-5/8
inches.

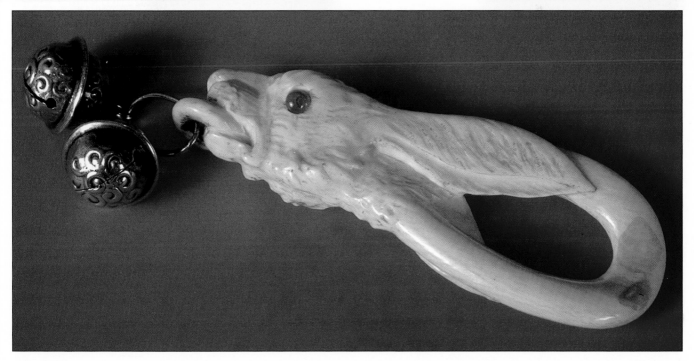

Fig. 144
Ivory teether, England, c. 1900–1910. Handle-shaped teether with a dog's head and two silver bells.
Length: 4 inches.

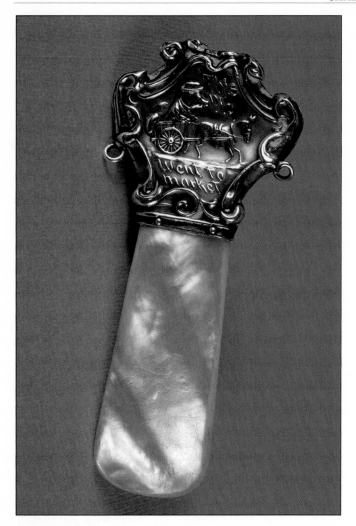

Fig. 146
Nursery Rhyme rattle, England, c.1910. Silver with pressed design of "This Little Piggy Went to Market." Some bells are missing. Mother-of-pearl stub handle. Birmingham mark. Length: 3-3/4 inches.

Fig. 148
Kate Greenaway storybook character teether, England, c.1900. Silver figure of little girl reading a book marked "ABC" and "XYZ." Two silver bells attached. She is mounted atop a nipple-shaped ivory teether. No marks. Length: 3 inches.

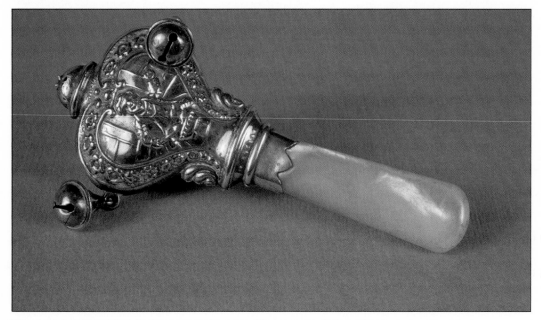

Fig. 147
Nursery Rhyme rattle, England, c.1910. Silver with stamped design of "Little Boy Blue." Has two silver bells and a mother-of-pearl handle. Birmingham mark. Length: 3-7/8 inches.

Fig. 149
Jester rattle, England, c.1900. Silver head of a jester or Punch with silver bells and a mother-of-pearl handle. The ring is missing. Birmingham mark. Height: 2-1/2 inches.

Fig. 150
Jester rattle, England, c.1900. Silver jester or Punch head with mother-of-pearl handle and an ivory ring. The bells are missing. Birmingham mark. Height: 3-1/4 inches.

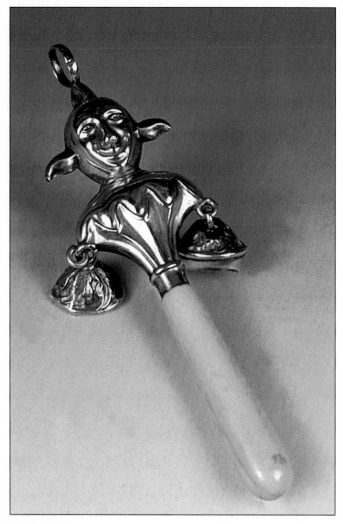

Fig. 151
Jester rattle, England, 1909. Stylized jester figure in silver with a whistle top, two bells, and a mother-of-pearl handle. Birmingham mark. Length: 3 inches.

Fig. 152
Sliding Monkey rattle, England, c.1900. Dumbbell-shaped rattle with pierced work knobs. Three-dimensional silver monkey arching its back slides up and down the rod. Two silver bells are attached at one knob. Has an ivory ring. Birmingham mark. Height: 4-7/8 inches.

rattles, including those made of gold or silver, became an accepted accessory for dolls in the early 1900s (Fig. 156). Queen Mary's doll house has toured the world for many years to raise money for British charities. It now reposes in the Bethnal Green Museum of Childhood in London. Queen Mary also collected the toy known as a *poupard*. It is a combination of doll, puppet, and rattle, very similar to the French *marotte*. It consists of a doll's head, usually of bisque, and a rounded body wearing a fancy costume. The whole thing was mounted on a stick. Bells or squeakers inside the body make a pleasant noise when shaken or twirled. A more complicated style is shown here (Fig. 157), where a clown's head is used, and his legs beat the drum.

As the twentieth century went on, new art styles emerged as a reaction against the decorative extravagance of the "Gilded Age" that preceded it. Simpler lines and motifs taken from natural forms were the basis of the works of William Morris and Charles Rennie MacIntosh among others. Art Nouveau, as this style is known, did not have great appeal to the conservative British public. While the new style had wide influence in the applied arts, jewelry, and architecture, Britons preferred traditional themes for their babies' toys. London bobbies, Scottish lassies, dogs, and dolls continued to be the most favored rattle motifs (Fig. 158, 159, 160, 161, 162, 163, and 164)

While Art Nouveau formed a bridge between Victorian style and the Art Deco period that followed World War I, the British public was not won over by Art Deco's sleek lines and minimal

Fig. 153
Dormouse rattle, England, c.1915. Silver mouse with long tail. Has an ivory ring. Closed rattle style with noisemakers inside and no bells. No marks. Height: 2-1/2 inches.

Fig. 154
Golliwog rattle, England, 1917. Silver figure of Bernice Upton's storybook character. The ring is missing. Birmingham mark. Height: 2-1/4 inches.

Fig. 155
Boy Scout rattle, England, 1912–1914. Silver Boy Scout in full uniform; the bells are missing. Has a mother-of-pearl handle. Birmingham mark. Height: 4-1/2 inches.

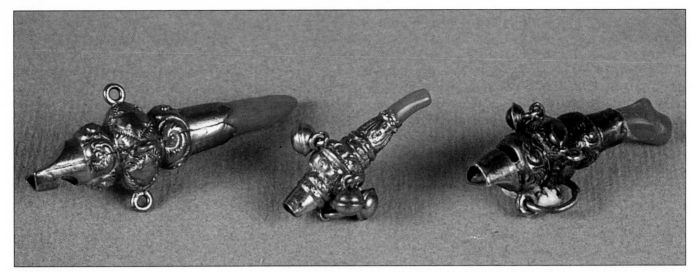

Fig. 156
Three Doll rattles, England, 1910–1915. Coral-and-bells in miniature; accessories for dolls and doll houses. Left: silver with whistle tip, length 1-1/8 inches; center: gold with whistle tip, length: 7/8 inch; right: gold with whistle tip, bells missing, length: 1-1/2 inches.

Fig. 157
Poupard rattle, England, early twentieth century. Clown with gauze and cotton costume, carrying brass cymbals and beating feet on paper drum. Hands and feet are wood. Bisque head is probably French or German. Sits atop a wooden stick. Height: 13 inches.

Fig. 158
London Bobby rattle, England, c.1915–1920. Silver-plated; the ring is missing. Height: 2-1/2 inches. Marked "EPNS."

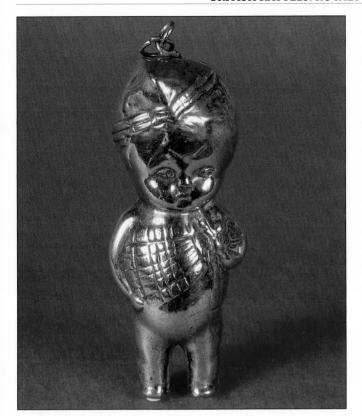

Fig. 159
Scottish Lassie rattle, England, c.1915–1920.
Silver-plated. Child in Scottish costume with tam
and tartan shawl. The ring is missing. Height: 2-3/8
inches. Marked "EPNS."

Fig. 160
Dolly rattle, England, c.1915–1920. Silver-plated
egg-shaped doll with bow ornament. Ring missing.
Height: 2-1/2 inches. Marked "EPNS."

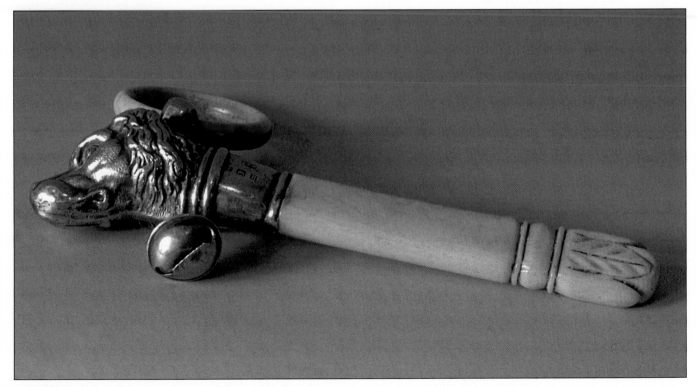

Fig. 161
Dog's Head teether, England, c.1920s. Silver spaniel head with one bell attached. Has a carved ivory
teething stick and an ivory ring. Length: 4-1/2 inches.

Fig. 162
Child's Head rattle, England, c.1910–1920. Silver head of boy, fully molded. Three bells are missing. Has a mother-of-pearl handle. There is a loop on top for a chain or ring. No marks. Height: 5 inches.

Fig. 164
Acorn rattle, England, 1917. Pierced silver acorn with ivory ring. Birmingham mark. Length: 2-1/4 inches.

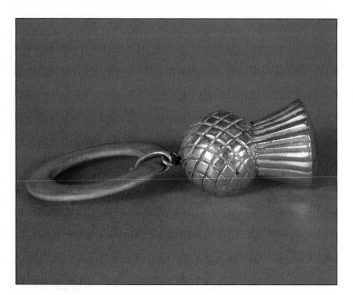

Fig. 163
Thistle rattle, England, c.1910–1920. Silver-plated thistle, the symbol of Scotland, on a bone ring. Height: 1-3/4 inches. Marked "EPNS."

Fig. 165
Celluloid rattle, England, c.1920s. Not a lamb, but a full-grown sheep! Although it is a rattle, it may have been part of a crèche scene. Length: 4-1/2 inches.

decoration. Many fine British artists contributed to the Art Deco style, including Clarice Cliff in pottery, for example, but in the aftermath of the horrible war, people sought the comfort of tradition in their homes, and in their children's toys. It was not until after World War II that England turned to modern design.

Less expensive and homemade toys, including rattles, had always existed in England. Celluloid rattles were imported from Japan before World War II and from China and Taiwan afterward (Fig. 165 and 166). Fathers continued to whittle and mothers continued to sew, making rattles that probably contented babies as much as silver ones did. Some folk art rattles of the time resembled American tramp art rattles. Others from this time period, like stuffed cloth rattles, may reflect wartime shortages (Fig. 167 and 168).

Rattles used in England today are very much like American ones. Dumbbells and small animals in silver are the most common types, and plastic rattles imported from the Far East are as easily found in Britain as they are in the United States.

With such a rich history in the arts, the British have remained true to their past. There seems to be a wide-spread nostalgia there now for the traditions of a safer age. The splendor of aristocratic life may have faded, but the standards set by the upper classes still permeate British society. A return to the styles of a bygone era is evident in the decoration and architecture of today. Interest has especially been revived in the applied arts of the Georgian and Victorian periods. Baby rattles, too, reflect this, for the British are producing copies of the antique rattles that once were handed down from generation to generation. The British remain proud of their heritage of coral-and-bells, a unique mixture of folklore, history, and craft.

Fig. 167
Folk Art rattle, England, early twentieth century. Carved wooden rattle similar in style to American tramp art. It may have been made by an itinerant farm laborer. Length: 5 inches.

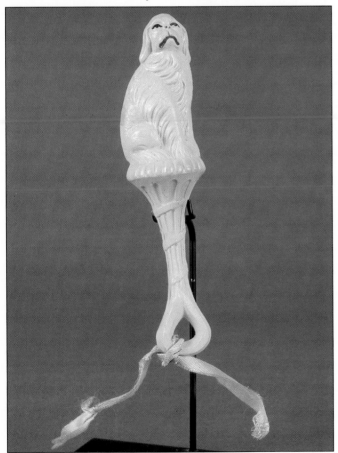

Fig. 166
Celluloid rattle, England, c.1920s. Molded spaniel with painted face atop a celluloid pedestal, which forms the handle. Height: 4-1/2 inches.

Fig. 168
Stuffed Doll rattle, Scotland, c.1940. Square cotton pillow with bells attached at corners. Has a painted doll face. 4-1/2 inches square.

Fig. 189
Postcard, France, postmarked
1903. The baby in a bassinet is
holding a painted tin rattle.
The card is a thank-you note
for a baby gift.

French Rattles and Teethers: Trinkets with Taste

France is a country fortunate in many ways, among them the geographical advantage of being in the very center of Europe. Although this location led to many wars with its neighbors, France was able to absorb the influences of the countries around it. With borders shared with Germany, Italy, and Spain, the French sampled the cultures of Europe and added their own flair for innovation and design. This is certainly true of baby rattles, called *hochets de bébé* in French.

French religious paintings from the Middle Ages showed the Madonna and Child with coral necklaces, and by the Renaissance period, coral and gold rattles appeared in these pictures. Churches and museums all over France have fine examples of the art of this kind.

Early French rattles relied heavily on Spanish and Italian models. These were usually of silver and were quite ornate. Many of them had the buttress-style scroll supports seen in the styles from Mediterranean countries. Crystal handles were often substituted for coral.

French taste became dominant throughout the courts of Europe during the time of Louis XIV in the early seventeenth century. French creativity flourished, especially in the applied arts of architecture, clothing, jewelry, and furniture. The French Goldsmith's Guild was founded in the late seventeenth century, and hallmarks were assigned to identify the place of origin and date of each piece. By the mid-eighteenth century the objects had the maker's name as well. These marks are very difficult to decipher on French rattles of the period. In addition to symbols, birds, flowers, fish, and articles of clothing were used as marks, French rattles also used a numbering system stamped in tiny squares. For the purposes of this book, only the fact that a hallmark exists on the rattle has been noted.

Marriages among the ruling houses of Europe led to close political alliances and the interchange of new ideas. Gifts were constantly exchanged between royal families, many of whom were closely related. Miniature paintings of eligible princes and princesses were sent out, and of

Fig. 169
Royal rattle, France, c.1780. Gold rattle in flower bud shape with an engraved gold handle. Reportedly a gift of the French court at the birth of Alexander I of Russia. Length: 5 inches. Courtesy the Florida International Museum, St. Petersburg, Florida.

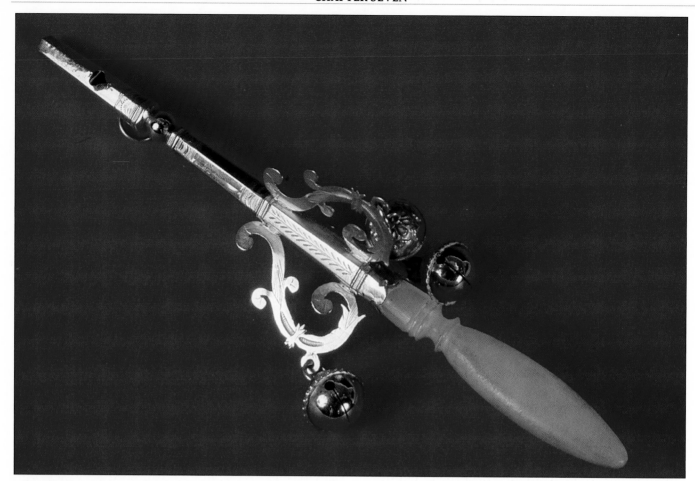

Fig. 170
Empire Period rattle, France, c.1803. Gold rattle with a scrolled buttress design, whistle tip, and an irides-cent mother-of-pearl handle. Has its three original bells. French hallmark. Length: 6 inches.

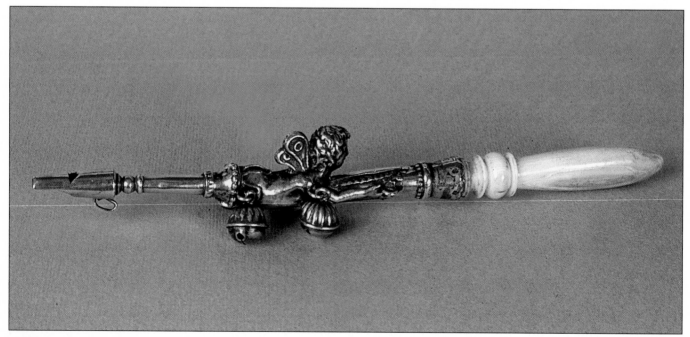

Fig. 171
Empire Period rattle, France, c.1800. Vermeil with ivory handle. Design is a reclining angel amid a cluster of bells. French hallmark. Length: 6 inches.

course, lavish gifts for newborn royal heirs were dispatched. For example, the King of France sent a gold rattle to the son of Alexander the First of Russia in 1780 (Fig. 169). And Napoleon's infant son, established as the King of Naples, was sent an elaborate gold rattle in the early 1800s.

The social and political reforms of French Revolution brought France a new simplicity in design. The Empire period shed the excesses of French court style, and echoed the restraint and elegance of the Georgian period in English art. After 1800, French baby rattles became lighter and simpler. Iridescent mother-of-pearl and ivory replaced coral handles on gold and vermeil rattles in many cases (Fig. 170 and 171).

Stamped and pressed metals came into general use about this time, and baby rattles were among the items made. The "Punchinelle" rattle shown here (Fig. 172) is an example which must have been made in large numbers because several identical rattles can be found in museum and private collections today. The silver Punchinelle, dated 1803, is in a tricorne hat, with a whistle atop it, and bells are attached to the coat. Other rattles of the Empire period developed a long, slender shape, topped by a whistle. Round-shaped rattle bodies, with or without bells, were positioned near the center of the rod. The handles were typically ivory or mother-of-pearl (Fig. 173, 174, and 175).

At the end of the Napoleonic Wars in 1815, hundreds of French sailors and soldiers were held in Britain in floating prisons or in detention camps. They earned pocket money by whittling or carving small objects in bone or ivory. These were sold at

Fig. 172
Punchinelle rattle, France, c.1800. Silver figure of hunchback clown, wearing Napoleonic period tricorne hat topped by a whistle. Several bells on the hem of the jacket are missing. Has a coral handle. French hallmarks. Height: 5 inches.

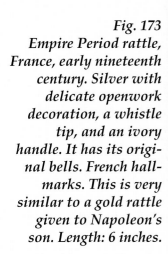

Fig. 173
Empire Period rattle, France, early nineteenth century. Silver with delicate openwork decoration, a whistle tip, and an ivory handle. It has its original bells. French hallmarks. This is very similar to a gold rattle given to Napoleon's son. Length: 6 inches.

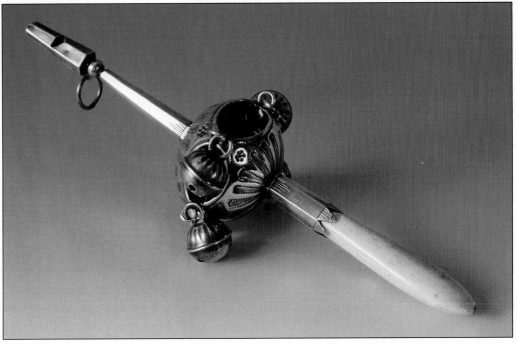

Fig. 174
Pierced-work rattle, France, 1830–1850. Vermeil; embossed and pierce-work decoration, with extended whistle tip, and an ivory handle. Length: 6 inches.

Fig. 175
Embossed rattle, France, c.1830–1850. Flattened circular shape in silver, with a whistle tip and its three original bells. Has an ivory handle. French hallmark. Length: 6 inches.

Fig. 176
Prisoner's Work rattle, France, early nineteenth century. Pierced and carved ivory of fine workmanship. Length: 5 inches.

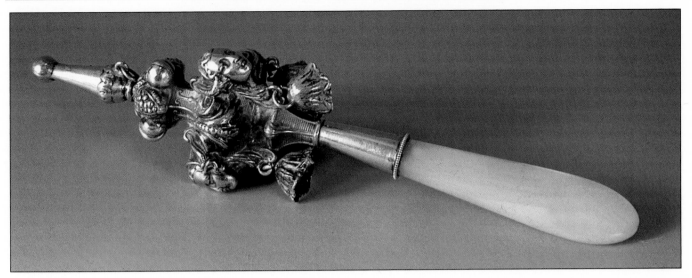

Fig. 177
Angel Faces rattle, France, mid-nineteenth century. Silver with tiers of bells and three-dimensional angel faces. Whistle tip and mother-of-pearl handle. French hallmark, probably Marseilles. Length: 6 inches.

Fig. 178
Spinner rattle, France, c.1840–1850. Vermeil with heavily decorated frame enclosing a full-ball spinner. Has a whistle tip and a mother-of-pearl handle. One bell is missing. Length: 5-3/4 inches.

Fig. 179
Spinner rattle, France, c.1840–1860. Silver ball held in embossed half-circle frame. No bells. Ivory handle. Length: 5 inches.

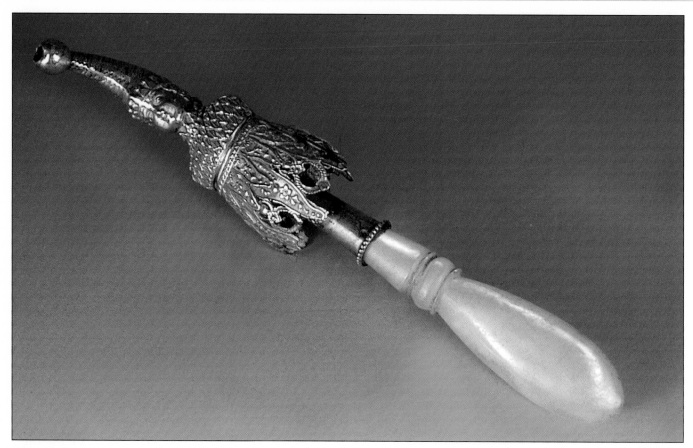

Fig. 180
Jester rattle, France, dated 1848 by Musée de l'Art Decoratif, Paris. Silver jester, wearing a tall hat with a whistle tip, in a costume that resembles tattered clothing. The costume's bells are missing. Has a mother-of-pearl handle. Length: 6 inches.

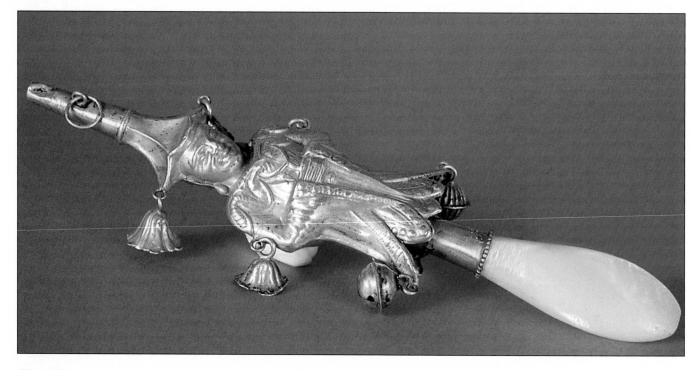

Fig. 181
Mandarin rattle, France, mid-nineteenth century. Silver; an interpretation of a Chinese gentleman, with a whistle atop his hat. Has its original bells and a mother-of-pearl handle. Length: 6 inches.

Fig. 182
Medieval Soldier rattle, France, mid-nineteenth century. Silver rattle of figure in cloak, probably St. Martin. This is one of the few religious personages depicted in baby rattles. The ivory ring and bells are missing. Has a whistle tip and a mother-of-pearl handle. French hallmark. Length: 5-1/2 inches.

weekly prisoner's markets in nearby towns, and exchanged for tobacco, needles, nails, and wire. Prisoners' work included small boxes, ship models, miniature guillotines, and spinning wheels, but their delicate baby rattles were among the most popular items (Fig. 176).

The reign of Louis Napoleon and the Third Empire in the early 1850s ushered in an era of opulence in French style. This period, which coincided roughly with the Victorian period in England, came to be known as *Belle Epoque*. Its influence continued to dominate European art for several decades.

In France, more substantial decorative details were added to furniture, clothing, and jewelry, and this embellishment can be seen in the baby rattles of the mid- to late-nineteenth century (Fig. 177). Spinner rattles, some with intricate openwork, came into fashion. Many were loaded with heavily wrought rigid frames and had handles made of ivory or mother-of-pearl (Fig. 178 and 179).

As the nineteenth century progressed, elements more attuned to popular taste began to appear in baby rattles. Figures such as jesters, and fantasy figures like the French idea of a Chinese mandarin made their debuts in baby rattles (Fig. 180 and 181). Although France was almost entirely a Catholic country, very few religious themes occur in rattles, but occasionally, a small religious medal was added to a rattle. The figure of St. Martin, who gave his cloak to a beggar, was probably meant more as a moral lesson of charity than as a religious

Fig. 183
Two French Horn rattles, France, 1860–1870. Silver with silver bells and whistle tips. Left has porcelain nipple in whistle end, diameter: 3-1/2 inches; right, diameter: 2-1/4 inches.

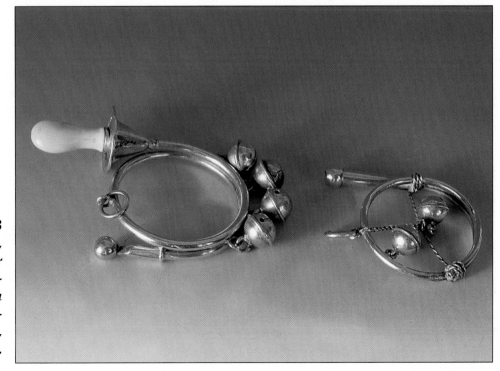

Fig. 185
Costume Plate, France, dated 1887. Color plate from **La Mode Parisienne,** *a fashion magazine of the period. Hand-colored print including an elaborately-dressed infant holding a coral-and-bells rattle. Width: 8 inches, height: 10 inches.*

icon (Fig. 182). Patriotic motifs are also scarce in French baby rattles, despite the great love of country the French people are known for. Baby rattles of the mid-nineteenth century also mirrored the pastimes of the upper classes. Hunting and its accessories played a big part in French country life, which is reflected in gun and hunting horn rattles (Fig. 183). France's colonies in West Africa provided ivory in abundance for teethers, rattles, and their handles and rings (Fig. 184).

In a French costume plate from 1887, an infant is shown holding a coral-and-bells rattle. By this time, the style had faded away, but this was probably the first type that came to the artist's mind when he imagined a baby holding a rattle (Fig. 185).

The *marotte* was introduced about 1900. As previously noted, this was a doll in fancy dress or jester costume with bells dangling from the skirt. The roundish body had a music box inside, and when whirled on its stick handle, a little tune would play and the balls would jingle. The doll heads were made of bisque, most of which came from Germany (Fig. 186).

Around this time doll rattles were in great demand. Often an entire set of three, consisting of a rattle for a child, one for a doll, and one for the doll house, was made with the same motif (Fig. 187 and 188). Doll rattles usually averaged about two inches in length, in proportion to a child's doll. The rattles used in doll houses were much smaller, some as tiny as five-eighths of an inch, so they would be the right size for a doll inhabiting the crib of a doll house.

Tin rattles were also common in the early 1900s. Tin rattles painted with scenes of children were a

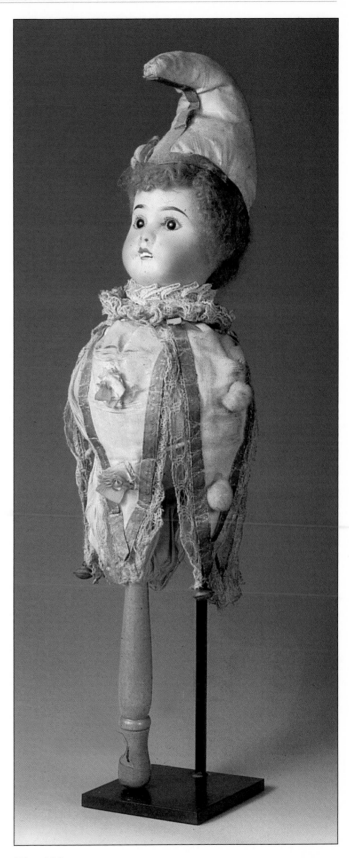

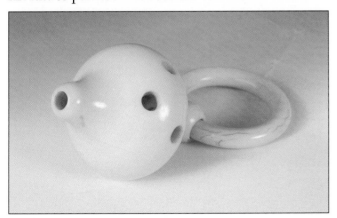

Fig. 184
Mammiform rattle, France, late nineteenth century. Modified ball of ivory with pierced design, a nipple-like mouthpiece, and an ivory ring. Length: 2-1/4 inches.

Fig. 186
Marotte, France, early twentieth century. Bisque-head doll in silk jester's costume with bells at the hem. A music box in the body plays when the toy is shaken. Wooden handle. Length: 13 inches.

Fig. 187
Set of Clown rattles, France, c.1900. Identical jester-head design on baby rattle, doll rattle, and dollhouse rattle. Silver-plated, each with ivory ring in proportion. Left: 1-1/2 inch diameter; center: 7/8 inch diameter; right: 2-1/2 inch diameter.

Fig. 188
Three doll rattles, France, c.1900. Left: pierce-work ivory rattle, length: 1-3/4 inches; center: openwork rattle of "pom-pom," the French equivalent of pinchbeck, a whistle tip and an ivory handle, length: 3 inches; right: pierce-work ivory rattle with a whistle tip and gold ring, length: 2-1/4 inches.

Fig. 190
Painted Tin rattle, France, c.1903. The colorful scene shows a child in a goatcart. This drum-shaped rattle has a tin handle and a porcelain whistle tip. Length: 6 inches.

Fig. 191
Painted Tin rattle, France, 1903–1904. Commemorates Blériot, an early French aviator, who flew across the English Channel in 1903. This drum-shaped rattle has a tin handle and porcelain whistle tip. Length: 6 inches

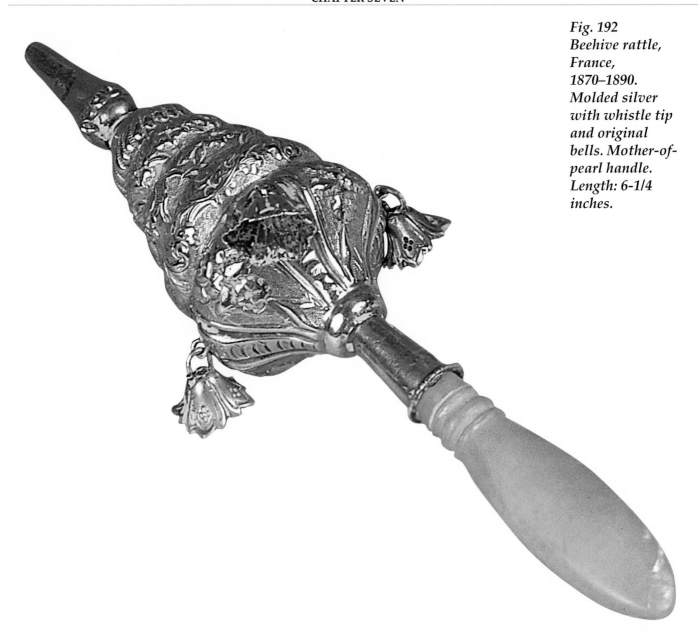

*Fig. 192
Beehive rattle,
France,
1870–1890.
Molded silver
with whistle tip
and original
bells. Mother-of-
pearl handle.
Length: 6-1/4
inches.*

popular style from this period. They usually had a tin handle, were drum-shaped, and had a porcelain whistle tip (Fig. 189, 190, and 191).

Sentimental motifs of flowers, beehives, cherubs, and the like continued to be made in ivory and silver at least until World War I, but other ideas were taking over in rattles and teethers (Fig. 192, 193, and 194).

Art Nouveau had entranced French artists from its beginnings in the 1890s. The posters of Alphonse Mucha and the early jewelry of René Lalique exemplified Art Nouveau. The simplified flowing forms found in nature captured the imagination of architects, graphic artists, jewelers, and decorators. Baby rattles soon followed the trend, and curvilinear lines and sinuous tresses were soon seen translated into rattles (Fig. 195, 196, and 197).

The next art style to emerge in Europe was called "Art Deco." The first exhibition to popularize Art Deco was held at the Musée de l'Art Decoratif in Paris in 1925. It electrified a world exhausted from a horrible war, a world that was ready to make fresh starts after the slaughter and deprivation of the war years. The simplified, streamlined shapes, minimal geometric decoration, and uncluttered lines promised a new world of serenity and elegance. Art Deco had among its practitioners Ellen Grey and Jacques Ruhlmann in furniture, Sonia Delaunay in textiles, and the later work of René Lalique in glass decorative objects. Baby rattles in Art Deco style in silver and ivory were made for most chic French babies (Fig. 198, 199, and 200). Although the style was copied for American babies at the time, it never caught on in

Fig. 193
Beehive rattle, France, early twentieth century. Embossed silver in bee and flower motif. Ring is missing; it was probably mother-of-pearl. Height: 2-1/4 inches.

Fig. 195
Art Nouveau rattle, France, c.1910. Silver bell with lily-of-the-valley design. Has an ivory ring. Height: 1-3/4 inches.

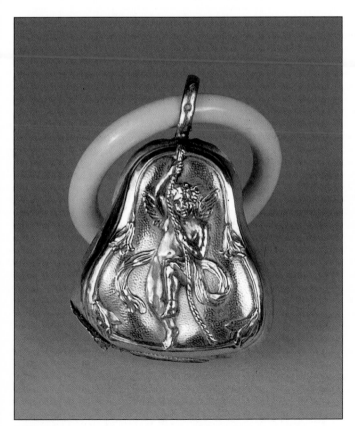

Fig. 194
Angel rattle, France, 1915–1920. Pressed silver design of an angel descending from heaven. Has an ivory ring. Height: 2-3/4 inches.

Fig. 196
Art Nouveau rattle, France, c.1910–1915. Silver with floral design in high relief. Has an ivory ring. Height: 2-1/2 inches.

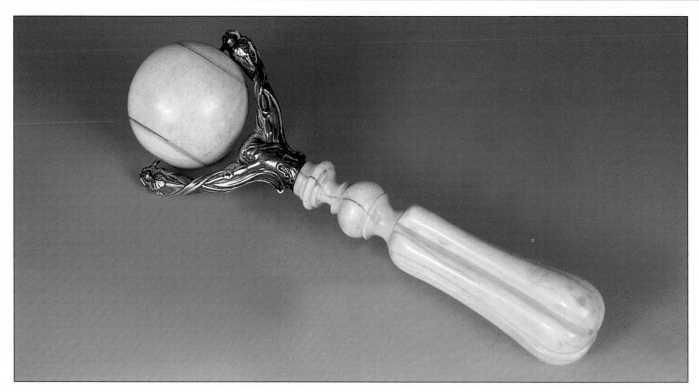

Fig. 197
Art Nouveau rattle, France, c.1910–1915. Spinner rattle. A woman's figure and arms in silver form the frame for an ivory ball. Has a carved ivory handle. Length: 5-1/2 inches.

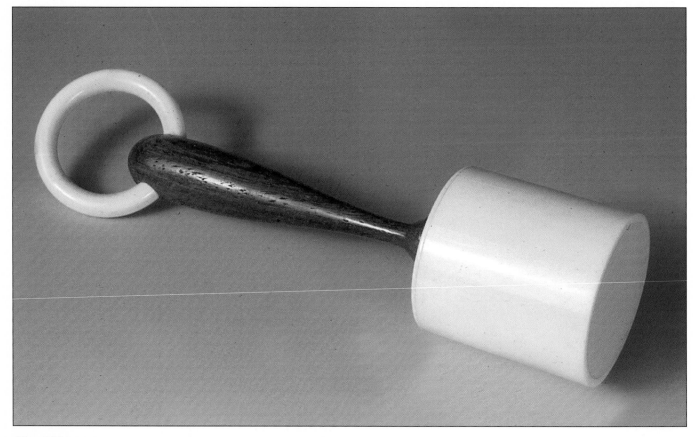

Fig. 198
Art Deco rattle, France, c.1925. Teak and ivory drum-shaped rattle. Attributed to Jacques Ruhlmann, who used knobs in this style on his furniture. Length: 6 inches.

Fig. 199
Art Deco rattle, France, c. mid-1920s. Silver rattle with typical geometric design of the period. Ivory ring. 1-1/2 inches square.

Fig. 200
Art Deco rattle, France, c. 1920s–1930s. Ivory in octagonal watchcase shape with ivory ring. Diameter: 2-1/4 inches.

Fig. 201
Costume Doll rattle, France, 1930s. Girl in Spanish costume, one of a series showing costumes of the world. Brightly painted plastic, with head and torso made of ping-pong balls. Length: 5-3/4 inches.

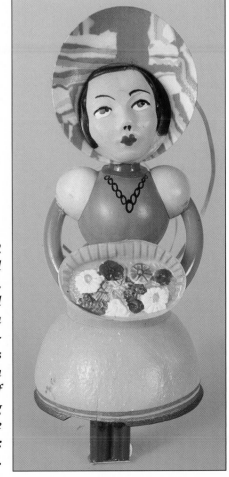

Fig. 202
Costume Doll rattle, France, 1930s. This doll is wearing a European peasant dress. This is another in the series of rattles showing costumes of the world. Height: 5-3/4 inches.

Fig. 203
World War II rattle, France, 1940s. Plastic ball rattle with painted design of a child wearing an American soldier's cap. Painted inscription "Sourire de France," meaning "French smile." Length 6 inches.

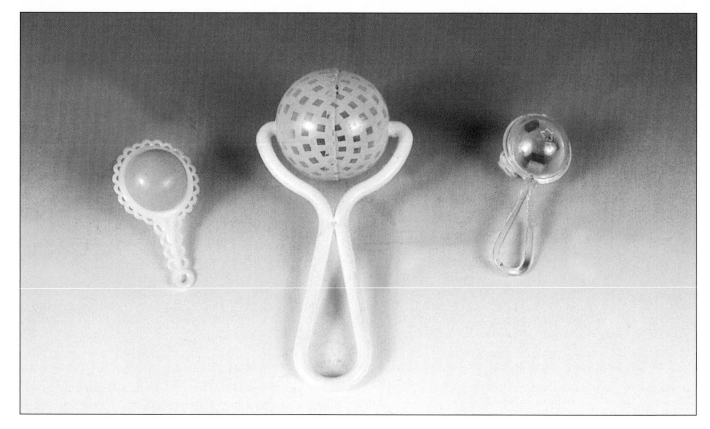

Fig. 204
Three Doll rattles, France, 1970s. Tiny spinner doll or dollhouse rattles in pink and white plastic. Left, height: 1 inch; center, height: 2 inches; right: height 1-1/2 inches.

Fig. 205
Group of modern French rattles, late twentieth century. This assemblage of wood and plastic rattles illustrates the continuity of rattle forms that have come down through history.

America. Most Art Deco rattles on the market today are French or Belgian.

In the 1930s celluloid rattles were imported to France from Japan, as were inexpensive toys from all over the world. But the French toy makers could not resist putting their own individuality even on disposable items. A series of costume doll rattles, representing the countries of Europe was fashioned from Ping-Pong balls, a novelty only the French could devise (Fig. 201 and 202)!

Although the production of luxury goods was suspended during World War II, American soldiers did not leave France without any souvenirs to take home to their children (Fig. 203).

Today's French baby rattles and teethers are very much like all the others in this homogeneous world. Plastics have taken over, even in the manufacture of doll and doll house rattles (Fig. 204). Some of the oldest forms of baby rattles, such as the clapper and the sistrum, are still being made in wood, though (Fig. 205). But we may leave it to the French artists to invent new and ingenious forms of baby rattles in the future. Vive La France! Vive *le hochet de bébé*!

Fig. 237
Oil Painting, Russia, mid-eighteenth century. Girl in fancy peasant costume is holding a silver rattle with animal-tooth or silver tooth-shape finial. Courtesy the Florida International Museum, St. Petersburg, Florida.

Other European Rattles and Teethers: Kings and Sea Monsters

Before the Napoleonic Wars (1793-1810), Europe was divided into small principalities and duchies, each influenced by one of the major powers: Spain, France, Turkey, and Russia. Marriages and political alliances among royal families created an almost uniform culture throughout Europe.

After Napoleon's defeat at Waterloo, the Congress of Vienna in 1815 rearranged the borders of Europe. The indigenous populations had to struggle to maintain their own identities. Folk art and court art were widely separated, and any baby rattles made by the peasants in their native folk styles have long disappeared.

It was a different situation among royalty, though. Gifts were constantly exchanged between the heads of states, many of whom intermarried. Artists and musicians moved freely from court to court bringing new styles and new ideas. A new royal heir was the occasion for a lavish gift, and baby rattles were pre-eminent among the items given. As has been mentioned earlier, the royal babies of France, Holland, and Russia were among the lucky recipients of these elaborate toys. Now let us look specifically at the baby rattles and teethers from some European countries.

Italy

In Italy, coral necklaces were shown on the Madonna and Child in religious paintings during the Middle Ages. Byzantine art also used coral in church decorations. By the Renaissance era, coral teething sticks with gold handles were depicted in church paintings, and from there it was but a few steps to add bells and a whistle. This novelty was treasured, and although very expensive, the coral-and-balls rattle became a favorite toy of children of the aristocracy all over Europe. As I have previously noted the belief in coral as a magical substance began in the Mediterranean region. In ancient Greek and Roman frescoes and jewelry, coral often appears, and may have been used in magic at far earlier times.

Secular paintings of children with rattles appear in Italy at the beginning of the sixteenth century. Santo di Tito, a Spanish-born painter who lived in Florence, was known for his portraits of children. One of his paintings from about 1570 shows a pierced-work gold rattle with a thick coral teether finial.

At the height of the Venetian power in Italy during the sixteenth and seventeenth centuries, rattles acquired a different form. There were innovations based on the whistles and bells mariners used for warnings at sea. Silver fantasy figures in

Fig. 206
Mermaid rattle, Italy, c.1700–1750. Lightweight silver mermaid with split fishtail. Three bells are missing. A silver chain is attached. Has a whistle tip. Height: 2-3/4 inches.

Fig. 207
Lion rattle, Italy, c.1750–1800. Stylized silver lion, the symbol of Venice, with a whistle at the mouth. The original bells and a silver chain are attached. The hallmark is unclear, but it has a Venetian stamping. Width: 2-1/2 inches.

Fig. 209
Painted Tin rattle, Italy, c.1914. Drum-shaped rattle with face of Christ; reverse side has head of a Pope, probably Benedict XV, who was Pope from 1914 to 1922. Has a painted tin handle and a whistle tip. Length: 6 inches.

Fig. 208
Hippocampus rattle, Italy, mid-eighteenth century. Silver figure, half-man, half sea-monster. High relief decoration with a whistle top and original bells. Italian hallmark. Width: 3-1/2 inches.

Fig. 210
Spinner rattle, Italy, c.1940s. Stylized silver ball spinner with a silver frame and handle, and an ivory ring. Length: 4-3/4 inches.

the shape of mermaids, lions (the symbol of Venice), and grotesqueries like the hippocampus (half-man, half sea monster) were popular (Fig. 206, 207, and 208). Coral does not seem to have been used in these silver rattles, except for occasional bead decorations. Seahorses were often the theme of the rattles, because dried seahorses were thought to be helpful to nursing mothers.

Italian rattles of the following few centuries interchanged and adapted designs from Spain and France. Religious themes in baby rattles are more common there than elsewhere, as can be seen on the tin rattle showing Christ on one side and a Pope on the other (Fig. 209).

Italy experienced only a modified interest in Art Deco in the 1920s and '30s. In modern times, Italian rattles follow international taste, with the plastic rattle being predominant. Silver and gold rattles made in the 1950s and '60s favor the pinwheel shape which is not too common in other countries. It seems to be an Italian innovation of the twentieth century (Fig. 210, 211, and 212).

Italian rattles are called *sonoglio*, which is a lullaby in itself!

*Fig. 211
Spinner rattle, Italy, c.1940s–1950s. Spinning gold wheel with gold wire frame and handle. Length: 5-1/2 inches.*

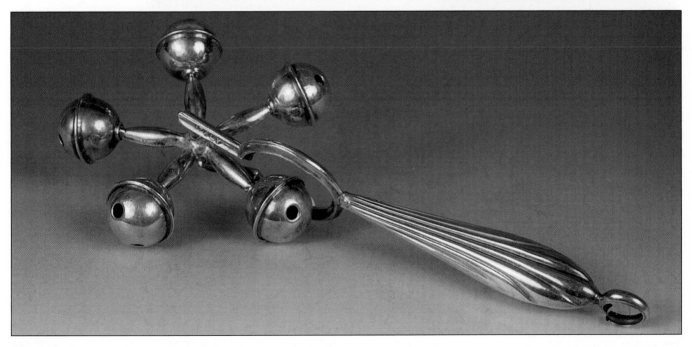

*Fig. 212
Pinwheel rattle, Italy, c.1950s. Silver pinwheel with five bells; a variation on the spinner rattle type. Silver handle. Length: 5-3/4 inches.*

Spain

Baby rattles were traditionally a part of the Spanish aristocrat's life, as pictured in paintings by Velasquez and Goya, among others. Adaptations of Venetian-style rattles—whistles, bells, and sea creatures—came to Spain at the beginning of the seventeenth century. Also, influences of everyday life became evident in baby rattles when hunting motifs, like horns and deer, showed up in the early seventeenth century (Fig. 213 and 214). Soon, influences from Northern Europe developed in baby rattles of the late seventeenth century. Intricate openwork designs and decorated bells were used, with crystal handles often replacing coral (Fig. 215). Coral-and-bells rattles, following English style, can be seen in Spanish paintings of children from the start of the nineteenth century.

Later nineteenth century baby rattles in Spain seem to have moved in step with the rattles of the rest of Europe. Clowns and jesters, bears, and rabbits took rattle forms very similar to those of France and England and continue to do so (Fig. 216).

The Moroccan and African heritage of Spanish culture is not ignored in baby rattles. Delicate filigree work in silver rattles and stylized African motifs prove that these influences are still important today (Fig. 217, 218, and 219).

Sound the *sonojero* for the baby rattles of Spain!

Fig. 214
Silver deer rattle, Spain or Spanish Colonial, seventeenth century. Leaping deer with bells on its feet, silver chains with amethyst finial attached. Width: 2-1/4 inches.

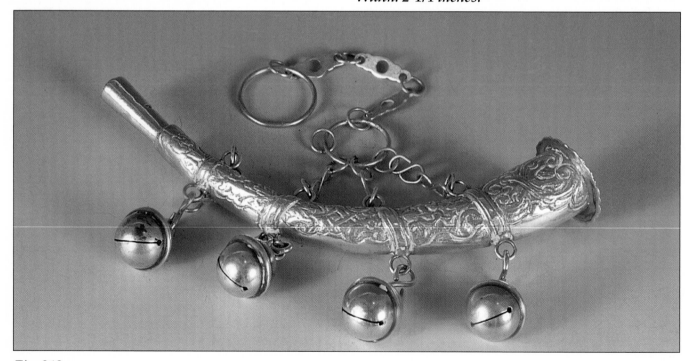

Fig. 213
Horn-shaped rattle, Spain, early seventeenth century. Heavily embossed silver, original bells, whistle tip. Suspended on a silver chain. Fig. 53 is probably based on a rattle of this period. Length: 6 inches.

Fig. 215
Openwork rattle, Spain, early eighteenth century. Silver openwork design with an elongated rod, whistle tip, and a short crystal handle. Length: 6-1/2 inches.

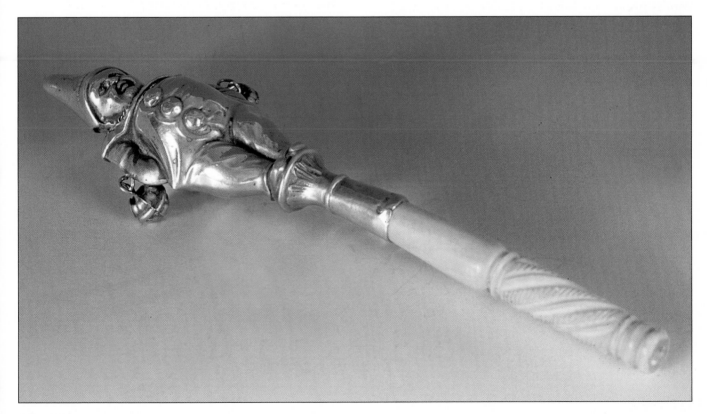

Fig. 216
Clown rattle, Spain, early twentieth century. Silver clown in high relief with two bells attached. The carved ivory handle is probably a replacement. The ring is missing. The hallmark is unclear. Height: 6-1/2 inches.

Fig. 217
Filigree rattle, Spain, c.1950. Silver spinner-rattle in Moroccan-style delicate filigree work. The ring is missing. Diameter: 2 inches.

Fig. 218
Pierced-work rattle, Spain, twentieth century. Silver with floral and pierce-work decoration. Modified ball shape. The ivory handle or ring has been replaced with an ivory bead. Diameter: 1-3/4 inches.

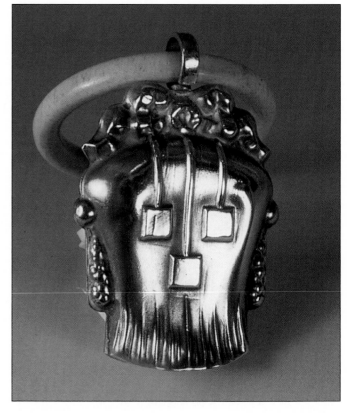

Fig. 219
African Head rattle, Spain, c.1950s. Silver-plated, with stylized African native head. Has an ivory ring. Height: 2 inches.

Fig. 220
Oil Painting, Holland, c.1635. Portrait of a richly dressed child carrying a large silver rattle with embossed and pierce-work decoration with an animal tooth finial. Attributed to Adnean van den Linde. Courtesy Lane Fine Arts, London.

Holland

Dutch rattles, called *rammelaar* or *rinkelbel*, have a long and fascinating history. The cultures of England, Spain (which ruled Holland for a long time), and Germany have combined to make a heritage rich and diverse. In the early portraits of children by Dutch artists, the northern influence is visible in the wolf's tooth used as the teether (Fig. 220 and 221). Spanish style prevailed while Holland was ruled by Spain, and crystal handles were used on the rattles then (Fig. 222 and 223). Dutch rattles, at times, even mirrored English styles and frequently copied them exactly (Fig. 224 and 225).

The coral-and-bells were in use in Holland by the mid-eighteenth century (Fig. 226 and 227). Dutch rattles with crystal handles reflect a Spanish style rattle. French inspiration can be seen in the vermeil open-ring rattle and teether in Fig. 228, which has a carnelian handle. Dutch colonies in Indonesia were also the source of motifs for baby rattles. The pagoda design of Fig. 229 was a reminder of Holland's world power.

For the remainder of the nineteenth century, Dutch rattles and teethers stayed close to other European models. Doll and doll house rattles were in fashion about 1900 (Fig. 230). Today, the baby rattles in wood, silver, and plastic sold in Holland do not differ greatly from all the others in Europe. There is even a Dutch manufacturer of silver Christmas tree ornaments who turns out copies of old rattles of the simpler Victorian period sort, such as bears, rabbits, and clowns.

Fig. 221
Oil Painting, Holland, mid-seventeenth century. Portrait of two young girls, one carrying a large silver rattle with an animal tooth finial. Possibly by the same hand as Fig. 220. Present whereabouts unknown.

Fig. 222
Crystal-and-bells rattle, Holland, early eighteenth century. Silver stem with seven original bells and a short crystal handle. Silver chain is attached. Length: 6-1/2 inches.

Fig. 224
Coral-and-bells rattle, Holland, c.1750. Silver hexagonal shape in the English style of George I with a thick coral handle, original bells, and a whistle near the tip. Length: 5-1/2 inches.

Fig. 223
Crystal-and-bells rattle,
Holland, early eighteenth
century. Silver bells and scrolled
buttress supports. Crystal
handle. Length: 5-1/2 inches.

Fig. 225
Regency-style rattle,
Holland, c.1830. Silver
with restrained decora-
tion and original bells.
The coral or crystal
handle is missing.
Length: 4 inches.

Fig. 226
Fire Screen, Dutch or Belgian, early eighteenth century. Painted wooden figure of a child carrying a coral-and-bells rattle. Painted wood trompe l'oeil figures like these were used to front fireplaces in warm weather. It may have been used in a nursery. Width: 23 inches. From the collection of Ides Cammaert.

Fig. 227
Crystal-and-bells rattle, Holland, 1749. Delicate gold stem and bells with a short crystal handle. The maker is unknown, but the rattle was made in Rotterdam. Length: 6-1/2 inches. From the collection of Mrs. Henriette Laverge

Fig. 229
Pagoda rattle, Holland, late nineteenth century. Silver rattle with two tiers of bells and a whistle near the tip. The style reflects the influence of the Dutch East Indies. The handle is missing. Length: 5-1/2 inches.

Fig. 228
Vermeil rattle, Holland, mid-nineteenth century. High relief embossed center ring, carnelian handle, four original bells, and a whistle tip. Length: 5-1/2 inches.

Fig. 230
Two Doll rattles, Holland, c.1900–1910. Silver or silver-plated in the form of acorns. Ivory rings. Left: 3/4 inch; right: 5/8 inch.

Belgium

Belgium, situated between France and Holland, absorbed the style of both countries, and early Belgian rattles were close in design to the Dutch ones. Art Nouveau became an important element in Belgian design at the end of the nineteenth century, and many artists adopted the style. The architecture of Victor Horta in Brussels attests to this style's popularity. Baby rattles, like the silver pear pictured here, also used the curved sinuous forms of Art Nouveau (Fig. 231). Art Deco, too, had its followers in Belgium, but did not achieve widespread acceptance there. The silver-plated rattle shown here is a rather ordinary interpretation of Art Deco style (Fig. 232).

Fig. 231
Art Nouveau rattle, Belgium, early twentieth century. Silver pear with embossed leaves. Ivory ring. Height: 3 inches.

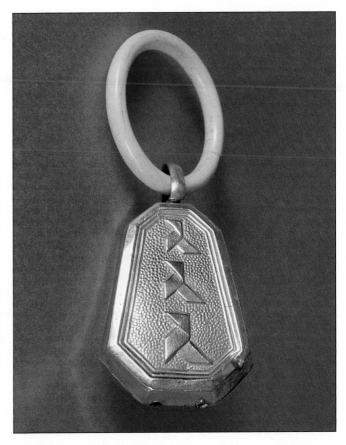

Fig. 232
Art Deco rattle, Belgium, c.1920s. Silver-plated with raised bowknot design. Height: 2 inches.

Germany and Austria

In Germany and Austria—where the rattle is known as a *Kinderrassel*—the rattle's design was modified and adapted to suit local tastes and customs. The rattles of the aristocracy throughout Europe retained the coral-and-bells type of rattle until well into the nineteenth century. However, the growing middle class brought its own taste to rattles, and peasant girls, butterflies, and alpine cottages were common motifs (Fig. 233, 234, and 235). A charming practice in Austria in the nineteenth century was to give an engaged couple a valuable coin as a gift. When the first baby arrived, bells and a chain were attached, making it into a rattle (Fig. 236).

Fig. 234
Butterfly rattle, Germany, c.1900. Silver with handsomely decorated butterfly wing motif. The handle is missing. Width: 2-1/2 inches. Gabrielle Roth Collection.

Fig. 233
Peasant girl rattle, Germany, c.1900–1915. Pressed silver of figure of girl in peasant costume holding a bunch of flowers. Has two bells, a whistle tip, and an ivory ring. Height: 5-1/2 inches. German hallmark.

Fig. 236
*Coin rattle, Austria, early twentieth century. The silver and silver gilt coin dates from 1750. The coin, called a **thaler**, is stamped with the face of Maria Theresa. Valuable old coins were given as engagement presents; the bells were added at the birth of the first child. Diameter of coin: 1-5/8 inches.*

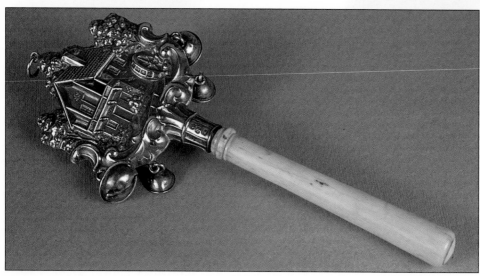

Fig. 235
Cottage rattle, Germany, c.1900. Silver, high relief design of typical alpine house with two bells and an ivory handle. Height: 6-1/2 inches. Munich hallmark.

Russia

Until the Russian Revolution in 1917, in Czarist Russia, the court and the nobles exchanged baby rattles with the other royal families of Europe, and a similarity of style resulted. Because coral was difficult to obtain, many of the Russian rattles used a wolf or boar's tooth as the teether, which was common practice in Northern European countries (Fig. 237).

An unusual example of Russian style is the set of baby jewelry shown here (Fig. 238). The set consists of a bracelet, a tiny ring, and a rod-like teether, all connected to a silver chain with bells attached. The ornaments are silver with niello decoration, characteristic of the silver work of the Black Sea area of Russia. Niello is a process of engraving silver and rubbing a dark metallic alloy in the design. The technique was used in the Renaissance, and has survived mainly in Russian silver work. Niello is also called "Tula" after the town that specialized in producing it.

Modern Russian rattles in woven straw are adaptations of the straw rattles that are made all over the world. Some have highly sophisticated and intricate patterns that make them very attractive (Fig. 239 and 240).

There is a lovely word for baby rattle in the Russian language: *po-grir-mushka*, sound that hushes a baby.

In modern times mass production and mass communication and transportation have made the world a much smaller place. There is a uniformity that has obliterated the national characteristics that existed earlier which made each country's culture unique. Today's European rattles, with some excep-

tions for local preferences, evince an international uniformity. During the 1920s and '30s, tin and celluloid rattles were imported into Europe from Japan. Now plastic rattles from China and Taiwan flood the toy market. Regrettably, the individuality, ingenuity, and the elegance of bygone days have vanished.

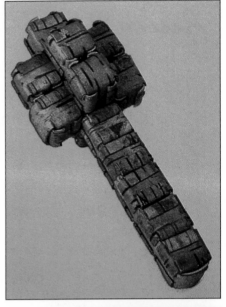

Fig. 239 Woven Reed rattle, Russia, c.1970s. Twisted straw design echoing basketry on rattles of many countries. Length: 4 inches.

Fig. 240 Woven Reed rattle, Russia, c.1970s. An intricately woven version of the classic straw rattle. Length: 4-1/2 inches

Fig. 238 Child's Ornament Set, Russia, c. 1900–1915. Silver bracelet, ring, and teether with niello decorations, hung on a silver chain, with bells attached. Length of chain: 14 inches; teether 2-1/2 inches.

Fig. 253
Woodblock Print, Japan, c.1880. One of a series of twenty-four prints by Miyagawa Shuntei called "Pastimes of Children." Height: 14 inches, width: 9-1/2 inches.

Asian Rattles, Flower Drums, and Palace Dolls

Baby rattles have been present in Asia for centuries. From their presence in religious rituals to their use as charms to protect children from harm, they have been and still are an important part of Asian traditions and customs. The most common Asian rattle form—the drum with banger—developed first in China, became the most prevalent style in all of the areas where Chinese culture was the chief influence, including Japan, Korea, and Taiwan as well as most parts of Indonesia.

The drum with banger, the traditional form of baby rattle that developed in China and, was in the shape of a small drum on a stick with external beads or bangers attached. The rattles were made of leather, paper, or sometimes silver, and were decorated with good-luck symbols of floral motifs. The drum shape has remained the prevalent style throughout Asia until the present day. Gourds and beads were also made into rattles for babies (Fig. 241). Teethers, made of ivory or wooden sticks strung together, appear in Chinese paintings of children at play. These teethers are very similar to scrimshaw crib toys and may have been the inspiration for clapper teethers of that type.

Other forms of baby rattles also appeared far back in Chinese history. An example exists from the Tuan period, c. 1280 A.D.—a small silver donkey with its legs bound together to make a circular form. The pebble or noisemaker is enclosed in the body of the animal. Silver rattles were made later in the form of small locks decorated with emblems of good fortune. These were sewn to a child's hat or clothing, as a precaution against wolves, and by extension, to keep away all evil that could befall a child (Fig. 242). Closed bell rattles, with similar decoration, which serve the same function are still being made today (Fig. 243 and 244). Traditions have a long life in China and these forms remained in use for many centuries.

Beginning in the late eighteenth century, the China Trade, as it was called, became an important segment of European imports. Along with silk and tea, porcelain was highly prized, and dinnerware was made in China to suit the needs of European tables. A high-fired white porcelain material, called *blanc-de-chîne*, was even made into a European-style baby doll rattle with outstretched arms and legs. Chips of porcelain inside the doll made it rattle—not a very practical idea for infants! If the child broke it, it could cause injury.

Fig. 241
Gourd rattle, China. Modern museum reproduction of an antique rattle with incised figures of the sages, which signify wisdom. Length: 2 inches.

Fig. 242
Lock rattle, China, late nineteenth century. Silver with embossed floral design. The lock symbolizes keeping the child safe from harm. Width: 1-3/4 inches.

Fig. 243
Bell rattle, China, early twentieth century. Classic Chinese bell shape in silver with floral decoration. Silver loop and semi-precious stone on top. Designed to keep evil away from a child. Height: 1-3/4 inches.

Fig. 246
China Export rattle, China, c.1900–1910. European style silver umbrella shape with vermeil decoration and bells. The ivory handle is missing. Length: 3-1/2 inches.

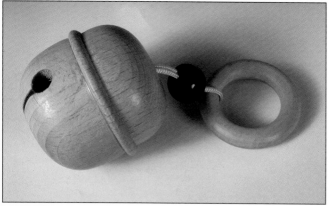

Fig. 244
Bell rattle, China, late twentieth century. Modern, bell-shaped, wooden. A wooden ring and a painted wooden bead are attached. This is another example of a rattle created to ward off evil. Height: 2-1/4 inches.

Fig. 247
China Export rattle, China, c.1900–1910. Silver in a flattened ball shape with floral decoration and dangling beads. The ivory handle is missing. This is another Chinese rattle created in a European style. Length: 3-1/4 inches.

Fig. 245
China Export rattle, China, mid-nineteenth century. Silver rattle in European style with floral engraving, three bells, and a carved ivory handle. Marked "MK" for Canton. Length: 5 inches.

Silver exports from China were also part of the fashion for exotic wares from the Orient that swept Europe in the nineteenth century. A wide variety of silver objects was produced including decorated opium pipes, bosun's whistles, tea caddies, and baby rattles. Chinese motifs were combined with European models, mainly from British sources (Fig. 245, 246, 247, and 248). Usually these rattles were based on versions of the coral-and-bells and clapper style, with ivory handles. These export rattles are rare and valuable today.

China today is known for making very inexpensive plastic rattles which are exported all over the world, but the traditional drum on a stick is still being offered in souvenir shops in San Francisco's Chinatown (Fig. 249).

Japan has had its own archaic art styles. Both the *Jomon* and the *Yayoi* cultures produced roughly fired and decorated clay figures and bowls. Small, doll-like sculptures with painted or incised designs have been found in archeological sites dating from the fifth to the third centuries B.C. Many of these figures have pebbles inside so they may have been used as ceremonial rattles or baby rattles, but their exact functions remain unclear.

In later times, much of the culture of Japan was adapted from Chinese traditions like the small drum on a stick with two bells or bangers attached. These were made in leather, wood, tin, and papier mâché (Fig. 250). To these borrowings, the Japanese added their own interpretations, superstitions, and skills to baby rattles, called *gara-gara* in Japanese.

Dolls have played an important role in the religious and secular life of Japan for many centuries. Elaborately dressed dolls representing the emperor and empress were given to children on

Fig. 248
China Export rattle, China, early twentieth century. Modified square shape in a European style with Chinese character for happiness engraved in center. Has two silver bells on a chain, a whistle tip, and an ivory handle. Length: 6-3/8 inches.

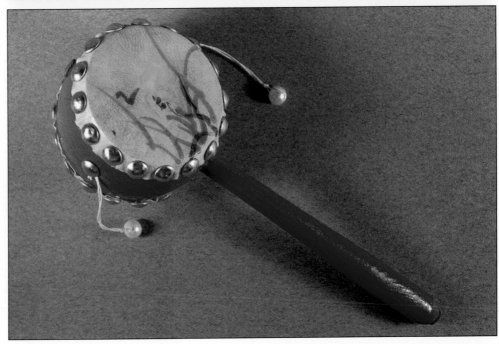

Fig. 249
Drum rattle, China, late twentieth century. Modern souvenir rattle in classic drum-on-a-stick Oriental shape. Painted leather with a wooden handle and pearl bead bangers. Length: 6 inches.

Boys' Day, a traditional holiday in the spring. The paper or cloth dolls given to children carried a rattle, drum, or bells, for it was believed the dolls were scapegoats which could attract evil away from the child. The bells were an added precaution to ward off evil.

Among the peasantry, straw rattles were woven to celebrate the rice harvest. These were shaped into small horses decorated with bells around the neck. Horses were symbols of prosperity in the Shinto religion. A mare with a colt promised good health for a mother and baby.

In the Edo period in Japan, late eighteenth to mid-nineteenth century, white porcelain costumed baby dolls were presented to the emperor's visitors. These "palace dolls," known as *gosho*, frequently held small musical instruments or a type of rattle called *den-den-taiko*. This was composed of three small drums with bangers vertically attached to a wooden stick (Fig. 251 and 252).

Fig. 250
Drum rattle, Japan, c.1840. Leather drum with bead clappers and a dark wooden handle. Length: 8-1/2 inches.

Fig. 251
Palace Doll with rattle, Japan, c.1850. White porcelain baby doll carrying a rattle composed of three drums with bead clappers on a vertical stick. Doll is 14 inches tall. Courtesy Michael Ayervais.

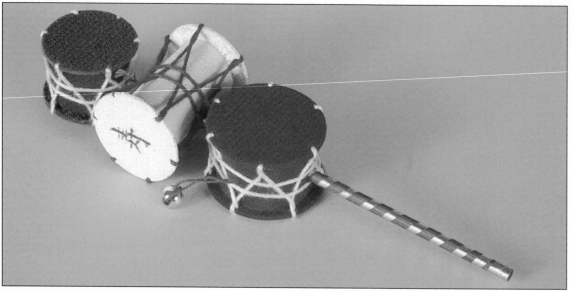

Fig. 252
Drum rattle, Japan, c.1980s. Modern papier mâché reproduction of rattle composed of three drums with bead clappers on a vertical stick. Height: 5 inches.

Baby rattles were often pictured in Japanese woodblock prints in the eighteenth and nineteenth centuries. Usually, they showed a mother with a baby on her back, carried in a cloth. The mother's arm was raised behind her, shaking the rattle to amuse the child (Fig. 253 and 254).

After Japan was opened to foreign trade in the late eighteenth century, Japanese baby rattles were occasionally made in silver, probably as gifts to foreigners. One of these, in the collection of Ides Cammaert, is in the form of a *daruma*. This is a popular Japanese toy, a demon with a pear-shaped body with a weighted bottom. It rolls back up when pushed over. *Daruma* were made in papier mâché, plaster, or wood.

In the 1920s and '30s, some Art Deco variations of the clapper style were made in Japan, but the drum-on-a-stick style prevailed (Fig. 255). Rattles in other forms, especially in celluloid, were made in Japan for export throughout this era (Fig. 256).

Between 1945 and the mid-1950s, objects made in Japan were required to be marked "Made in Occupied Japan." Ivory figurines, porcelain tea

Fig. 256
Rabbit rattle, Japan, c.1930s. Brightly colored celluloid in a typical example of rattles exported to Europe from Japan (it was purchased in France). Height: 4-1/2 inches.

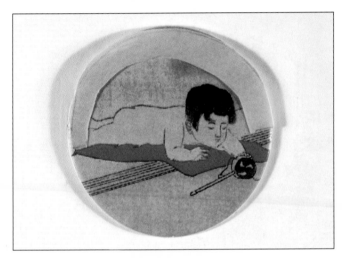

Fig. 254
Child with rattle, Japan, c.1880. Detail of wood-block print, showing child playing with a traditional drum-shaped rattle with an attached bell or beads.

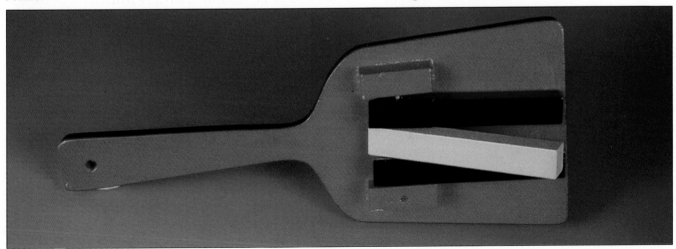

Fig. 255
Art Deco-style rattle, Japan. Brightly painted wood in a version of the clapper style. Length: 6 inches.

Fig. 257
Santa Claus rattle, Japan, 1945–1955. Celluloid rattle of Santa, marked "Made in Occupied Japan," intended for the American market. Santa has a face reminiscent of the Japanese sage who symbolizes long life. Height: 4-1/2 inches.

inches.
Fig. 259
Painted Faces rattle, Japan, c.1970s. Seven clay bells with painted faces strung on a cord. Purchased at the Tokyo Folk Art Museum. Diameter of each bell: 3/4 inch.

Fig. 258
Tambourine rattle, Japan c.1970s. Has six clay bells with painted faces attached to a rigid straw-wrapped frame. Purchased at the Kurashiki Folk Art Museum. Diameter: 6-1/2

Fig. 260
Drum rattle, Japan, c.1970s. Classic papier mâché drum rattle with painted stylized cat design and two clappers. A miniature drum is set atop rattle, which is on a wooden

sets, and many other decorative items were made during the American occupation. Included among these were baby rattles like the celluloid Santa shown here, which has a decidedly Oriental face (Fig. 257). "Made in Occupied Japan" pieces command high prices from collectors today.

Hand-crafted items are part of Japan's long heritage, and there has been a revival of interest in these ancient traditions in the late twentieth century. Japan's many folk art and craft museums exhibit both modern and antique toys, baby rattles among them, and often the newly crafted rattles are for sale there. Painted clay rattles echo classic, early rattle forms of the tambourine and beads on a string (Fig. 258 and 259).

Many types of baby rattles are currently being manufactured by toy companies in Japan, largely for home use. The Japanese have resisted the tendency to produce cheap plastic rattles for their own children. In general, they have remained true to natural materials and familiar forms. Papier mâché, cloth, and wood are the most frequently used materials and traditional themes remain popular (Fig. 260, 261, 262, and 263).

Dolls and horses, cats and monkeys continue to delight Japanese children, and perhaps the quality of their rattles helps to establish a regard for excellence in their future lives.

In the Far East, society on the whole has held fast to traditional values. Even with the extreme changes in the political system of China, and the emergence of modern Japan as a world power, allegiance to the old ways of life still continues. Partially this is due to the respect for ancestors, which leads to a reverence for the folkways and the customs of the past. These include the heritage of the drum-and-banger-style of rattles, and the many charms and superstitions related to child-rearing in China and Japan.

stick. Length: 8 inches.
Fig. 261
Doll rattle, Japan, 1985. Silk or rayon printed cloth cover a ball rattle with the painted hair and face of a typical Japanese doll. Purchased at the

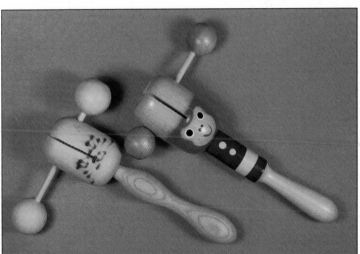

Okayama Prefecture, Japan. Length: 7 inches.
Fig. 263
Two Wooden rattles, Japan, 1980s. Side-to-side clapper-style modern rattles. The cat and the monkey are commonly portrayed in Japanese toys. Length: 4-1/2

Kurashiki Folk Museum.
Diameter: 2-1/4 inches.

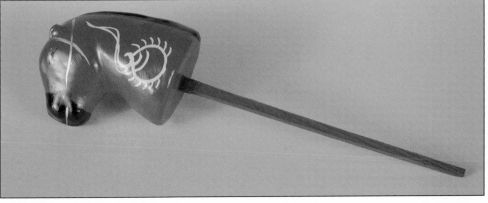

Fig. 262
Hobby Horse rattle, Japan, 1970s. A papier mâché horse head is attached to a wooden stick. Purchased in

Fig. 271
Sea Horse rattle, India, mid-twentieth century. Silver; adaptation of a European design with a whistle tip and silver bells. Length: 6 inches.

Indian Rattles
"...rings on her fingers and bells on her toes"

Baby rattles in India, called *chankna*, have been in use since the archaic period (1000 B.C. to 300 B.C.). Archaeologists excavating around the country in modern times have discovered small unpainted clay rattles in the form of dwarves, goblins, and animals. Many of these have been found in the Chandraketugarh area of eastern Bengal, dating from the second to first centuries B.C. (Fig. 264).

Later times saw the emergence of organized religious practices, and a full panoply of deities and rattles appeared as the symbols and appurtenances of a god figure. In some of the many guises of Lord Shiva, chief Hindu deity, a rattle in the shape of a double-headed mallet is shown in his hand. Because Shiva represented good fortune, this form was often adapted in baby rattles (Fig. 265). Rattles, along with bells, were also used in temple rites and dances and in orchestras.

A typical element in Indian design is the addition of small bells or jingling clusters of beads to jewelry, dance wands, and temple regalia. This, of course, can also be seen in baby rattles (Fig. 266 and 267).

Fig. 264
Archaic Period rattle, India, second to first century B.C. Terra-cotta elephant with traces of kaolin. From the Chandraketugarh region. Height: 5-1/2 inches.

Fig. 265
Mallet rattle, India, early twentieth century. Silver; in the style of traditional symbol of Shiva, god of good fortune. Low relief decoration with clusters of small beads attached. Length: 6-1/4 inches.

Silver has always held a role of great importance in Indian life. Brides and grooms are literally laden with gifts of silver coins and jewelry. It follows that silver baby rattles are also traditional gifts, although ivory and gold teethers and rattles are sometimes offered as well (Fig. 268). Dumbbell and ball shapes are commonly used (Fig. 269). Regional styles, such as the inlaid ivory work characteristic of Jaipur, are also reflected in baby rattles (Fig. 270).

The presence of the British in India for almost two hundred years (1750-1947) left its mark on upper caste Indian culture. Adaptations of English furniture, jewelry, and table silver were highly prized and copied. Rattle styles, too, were borrowed from British models, as can be seen in the silver seahorse, a modern version of a buttress rattle, freely based on an antique British example (Fig. 271).

Rattles which serve a dual purpose often appear in India. Made of brass or other base metals, objects like foot-scrapers, combs, hairpins, and rings with bells attached were transformed

Fig. 266
Ball-shaped rattle, India, early twentieth century. Silver with relief floral decoration and six clusters of small beads. Length: 5-3/4 inches.

Fig. 267
Fringed rattle, Nepal, early twentieth century. Silver with embossed design and silver chain fringe. Has a silver handle with a whistle tip. Length: 5-3/4 inches.

Fig. 269
Ball rattle, India, early twentieth century. Silver in flattened ball shape with intricate pierced-work design and a silver bead inside. Diameter: 2-1/2 inches.

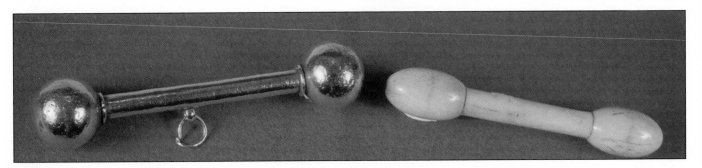

Fig. 268
Two small teethers, India, c.1900. Narrow rods with knobbed ends in a modified dumbbell shape. Left: gold, with ring for chain or cord, length 2-7/8 inches. Right: ivory, length: 2-3/4 inches.

into rattles (Fig. 272). They allowed the mother to keep her hands free for work, while the baby on her back was amused by the tinkle of the bells.

Today's Indian rattles are often homemade and follow the painting styles of the individual regions. A stuffed cloth rattle comes from the Orissa area in South India (Fig. 273). The style can be easily identified by the design and colors characteristic of the region. The sistrum-type rattle, although made in 1997, is a very close relative of one of the original prototype rattle forms of antiquity (Fig. 274).

Although India continues to develop rapidly as a modern industrial country, it has not abandoned its roots. Skilled craftsmen continue to create objects with a sensitive fusion of yesterday and today.

Fig. 273
Stuffed cloth rattle, India, c.1970. Cloth doll with beads or pebbles inside, brightly painted in typical Orissa face and costume style of South India. Height: 9 inches.

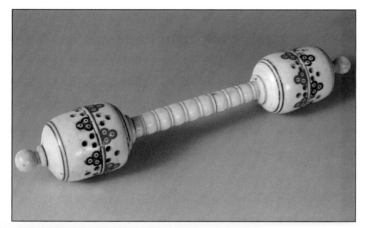

Fig. 270
Dumbbell rattle, India, c.1910. Ivory with inlaid multicolored decoration, typical of the Jaipur area. Length: 5 inches.

Fig. 272
Foot scraper rattle, India, twentieth century. Brass with a scored and weighted bottom. A bird and rabbit are on top. Width: 3 inches.

Fig. 274
Sistrum rattle, India, 1997. Sistrum with wooden frame and brass discs in a classic form. Height: 9 inches.

Fig. 283
Gourd rattle, Argentina, early twentieth century. The gourd is bracketed with decorative silver castings on the top and bottom. Height: 4 inches. From the collection of Ada Ghiron Segal.

Baby Rattles from Around the World

From Timor in Indonesia to Timbuktu in Africa, baby rattles of all sorts have been made and used from time immemorial. This chapter gives a sampling of the similarities and differences in how a diversity of cultures has interpreted this simple toy.

In Latin America, a rich tradition of producing baby rattles dates back to Pre-Columbian times. Archaeological sites throughout the Americas have yielded small clay figures of animals, fruits, and birds with pebbles or seeds inside which were certainly used as baby rattles. Central America, especially Costa Rica and the surrounding areas, has given scholars ancient objects which show the life of the period. Among these are painted and molded baby rattles that date from the eleventh to fourteenth century A.D. Earlier examples, in somewhat cruder form, have also been excavated (Fig. 275, 276, and 277).

Mexico, too, has provided a number of interesting forms of baby rattles. Examples dating from the Late Classic Maya period (running from the tenth century to the fourteenth century A.D.) have been found like the terra-cotta rattle featured here (Fig. 278). The resurgence of Mexican silver crafts in the 1940s and '50s produced several individual silversmiths whose work has become treasured and collected (See Fig. 44). The most famous workshops were centered in Taxco and included those of Los Castillos and William Spratling.

Among the present-day folk art rattles made in Mexico are papier mâché skulls, commemorating the Day of the Dead, *Dia de los Muertos*, a holiday fusing Catholicism with the earlier pagan religion of the country (Fig. 279).

The contemporary folk art rattle from Guatemala shown here seems to have been made of objects found around the house and gaily painted with the face and figure of a local hero or saint (Fig. 280).

Fig. 275
Pre-Columbian rattle, Costa Rica, eleventh-thirteenth century A.D. Polychromed terra-cotta in the form of a mythic animal. Height: 3 inches.

Fig. 276
Pre-Columbian rattle, Costa Rica, eleventh-thirteenth century A.D. Terra-cotta bird head on rounded body. Height: 3 inches.

Fig. 277
Pre-Columbian rattle, Costa Rica, c. fourteenth century A.D. Terra-cotta pepper or gourd form. Height: 2-1/2 inches.

Fig. 278
Pre-Columbian rattle, Mexico, tenth-fourteenth century A.D. (Late classic Maya). Terra-cotta ball with incised and pierced decoration. Diameter: 2-1/4 inches.

Fig. 279
Papier Mâché rattle, Mexico, 1994. Painted skull head, typical of toys made to celebrate the "Day of the Dead." Has brass stud eyes and is on a wooden stick. Length: 8 inches.

Woven straw rattles are typical of the basketry work of Amazon Indian tribes of Brazil. For example, the little man pictured here has exceptionally fine weaving and brass bells attached (Fig. 281). It was collected among the Arequipa Indians in 1895.

Other South American countries followed traditions of their own. In Ecuador, the Jivaro Indians sew shells to a narrow strip of cloth to serve as a baby rattle. The ancient Incas in Peru made painted pottery or gourd baby rattles with symbolic feline designs (Fig. 282).

During the colonial period in Central and South America, settlers from Spain and Portugal kept close cultural ties with the mother countries. Most of their luxury goods were imported, including baby rattles, and brought to the new world the styles currently fashionable in Europe, but sometimes local craftsmen made versions using local materials like gourds and precious metals (Fig. 283).

In the Middle East, baby rattles and teethers customarily have been constructed of stick teethers connected to bells on a chain. In Turkey, on the borders of the Black Sea, a Russian influence is evident in the silver niello work and the long teardrop shape of the teethers. The Berbers of North Africa traditionally make baby rattles consisting of five silver bells on a chain, representing the five fingers of Fatima. Variations of these forms are prevalent all over the Middle East and follow centuries-old forms and customs.

Many parts of the world have not had sophisticated and elaborate trinkets and rattles for their babies, but the protection of children from the evil eye and magic spells has always been a constant concern everywhere. In East and West Africa, Southeast Asia, and the Pacific Islands, dance and Shamanic rattles were an integral part of religious and ceremonial life, and baby rattles were made as well. Most of these were made of hemp, shells, gourds, and basketry and were adorned with

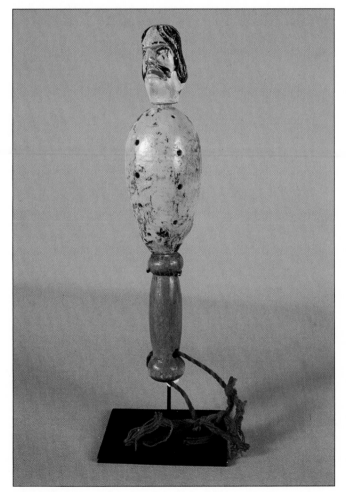

Fig. 280
Folk Art rattle, Guatemala, 1950s. Brightly painted wooden rattle made of household objects with the face of a saint or local hero. Length: 8-1/2 inches.

Fig. 281
Basketry rattle, Brazil, collected from an Amazon tribe in 1895. Woven straw man with a painted face and brass bells. Height: 6-1/2 inches (plus a 4-inch wooden handle).

Fig. 282
Gourd rattle, Peru, c.1970s. This is a museum replica of a Pre-Columbian Indian rattle with a painted feline face and markings. Length: 3 inches. From the collection of Bernice Hantman.

Fig. 285
Twisted straw rattle, Kenya, 1996. Traditional woven style, painted in bright colors. Length: 5-1/2 inches

Fig. 284
Gourd rattle, Ivory Coast, Africa, early twentieth century. Low relief crocodile design on one side and a human face on the other. From an Akan tribe. Diameter: 4-7/8 inches.

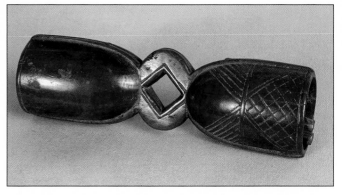

Fig. 286
Double-drum rattle, Zaire, Africa, first half of the twentieth century. Polished dark wood with an incised design and wooden clappers. Made by the Kongo peoples. Length: 5 inches.

Fig. 287
Drum rattle, Thailand, c.1970s. Bright colored paper on a bamboo frame with bead clappers and a wooden handle. Its purpose is to ward off evil. Diameter of drum: 2-1/2 inches.

Fig. 288
Cowrie shell rattle, Philippines, early twentieth century. Clustered cowrie shells attached to hemp rope. Length: 4 inches.

fetishes and charms. Because these materials were perishable, few have survived.

In East Africa, gourds with incised tribal or animal motifs are used for baby rattles (Fig. 284). Beads, shells, and the hoofs of small deer are sewn to a child's clothing as amulets and charms. Woven straw rattles, used in tribal dances, were commonly made in similar form for children and continue an ancient tradition (Fig. 285).

West African religious practices also included rattles and charms of many kinds. The small drum rattle with open ends and clappers inside is a minia-

Fig. 289
Folk Art rattle, Indonesia, mid-twentieth century. Carved wooden sticks with geometric decoration strung on a woven raffia cord. Length: 2-1/2 inches (each piece).

ture of a typical West African drum form (Fig. 286).

In Nigeria, mothers attach rings and bells to a sick child's clothing to prevent demons from re-entering the child's body. This practice was believed to cure the illness and drive away malevolent spirits.

The art and beliefs of China were a major influence on the cultures of Thailand, Vietnam, and Burma. Chinese customs continue to dominate many aspects of Southeast Asian life. The Chinese rattle of a drum on a stick with bangers is found, with some variations, throughout this area. It is also common practice to sew bells, coins, and beads on a child's hat or clothing to keep away evil (Fig. 287).

Baby rattles from the Pacific Islands, including the Philippines, were often made out of highly valuable cowrie shells. These were modifications of the rattles used in dances and ceremonies (Fig. 288). In Indonesia, rattles from the outer islands echo one of the oldest types of rattles—wooden sticks strung on a cord. This simple combination makes a very pleasant sound and is safe and can be easily replaced (Fig. 289).

Another common example of a double-duty rattle is a butter churn rattle like the one pictured here (Fig. 290). This carved wooden rattle from Nepal is the top of a yogurt or yak butter churner. The pleasant sound it made while being whirled amused the baby carried on the mother's back.

Despite all the ethnic diversity, differences in customs and attitudes toward child-rearing, people all over the world share the universality of giving their babies a toy that comforts, protects and amuses them—baby rattles.

Fig. 290
Butter Churn rattle, Nepal, early twentieth century. Carved wooden handle of a yak butter churner with a wooden ball inside. Length: 4-1/2 inches.

A Last Word

Hopefully, this book has inspired you to consider collecting baby rattles and teethers. Here are a few thoughts to keep in mind: Think before you buy, trust your dealer (if you have found a good one), and don't be afraid to take a chance once in a while. You will regret the pieces you lost by being over-cautious!

As you go on collecting, you will learn a lot about the lives of many peoples from times gone by. You will learn about the skill and ingenuity of craftsmanship, both antique and modern. You will get to meet some interesting people, and you will acquire a sense of the human heritage behind the effort of protecting, amusing, and comforting children with rattles and teethers.

Despite the competition from other areas of collecting, baby rattles still represent a rewarding field to explore. As yet, there are not too many people who collect them exclusively. The beginning collector will have no difficulty finding prime examples and interesting curiosities in the search for baby rattles and teethers. At flea markets and bazaars, antique shows and second-hand toy stores, and wherever baby-related objects can be found, treasures await.

Good hunting!

Price Guide

The prices in this guide are conservative retail prices—what a collector might expect to pay for a rattle or teether in an antique shop or antique show or mall. Prices for antiquities, historical objects, or for pieces in museum and private collections are not included, but recent auction and dealer prices are.

No.	Description	Provenance	Date	Price
2	Archaic Rattle	India	2nd-1st century B.C.	$1,500
5	Pre-Columbian Rattle	Mexico	c.1200 A.D.	$800
7	Coral-and-bells Rattle	England	c.1719	$1,200
9	Coral-and-bells Rattle	England	c.1830	$900
10	Art Nouveau Rattle	U.S.	c.1900-1910	$85
11	Art Deco Rattle	France	c.1925	$75
12	Golf Rattle	U.S.	c.1935-1940	$20
13	Adult Pacifier	U.S.	1982	$10,000
14	Adult Rattle	U.S.	1996	$100
15	Gourd Rattle	Kenya	c.1970	$4.00
16	Drum Rattle	U.S.	1990	$8.00
17	Scrimshaw Rattle	U.S.	c.1840	$450
18	Dumbbell Rattle	U.S.	c.1910	$60
19	Twisted Straw Rattles	Various	20th century	@ $10
20	Folk Art Rattle	U.S.	1980s	$8.00
21	Coral-and-bells Rattle	England	c.1740	$950
22	Jester Rattle	England	1909	$100
23	Teething Ring Rattles	U.S.	early 20th century	$45 and $55
24	Celluloid Rattle	Germany	c.1920s	$35
25	Sistrum-type Rattle	U.S.	1910	$125
26	Spinner Rattle	U.S.	c.1940s	$40
27	French Horn Rattle	France	c.1920s or '30s	$100
28	Whimsy Rattle	U.S.	late 19th century	$85
29	Crib Toy	U.S.	1930s	$80
30	Woven Straw Rattles	Various	1990s	@ $10
31	Coral-and-bells Rattle	England	mid-19th century	$600
32	Ivory Rattle	France	early 19th century	$350
33	Heart Rattles	U.S.	late 19th century	@ $40-$60
34	Celluloid Rattle	U.S.	1920s	$15
35	Bakelite Rattle	U.S.	1940s	$85
36	Tin Rattle	U.S.	late 19th century	$70
37	Clown's Head Rattle	U.S.	unknown	$10
38	Alphabet Rattle	U.S.	c.1950	$2.00
39	Artisan's Rattle	U.S.	1990	$45
40	Miniature Painting	England	c.1830	$2,500
41	Paper Doll Book	Germany	c.1908	$25
42	Toy Gun Rattle	France	mid-19th century	$550
43	Minnie Mouse Rattle	U.S.	c.1930s	$30
44	Taxco Rattle	Mexico	c.1940-1950	$100
45	Coral and Gold Teether	England	1775	$3,500
46	Victorian Rattle	England	c.1875	$150
47	Umbrella Lady Rattle	France	late 19th century	$200

48	Umbrella Lady Rattle	France	late 19th century	$250
49	Dumbbell Rattle	France	c.1900	$225
50	Reproduction Rattle	U.S.	c.1990	$35
51	Reproduction Rattle	U.S.	c.1980s	$45
52	Reproduction Rattle	England	1990s	$35
53	Sea Monster Rattle	Spain	1980s	$100
54	Reproduction Rattle	Spain	1980	$55
55	Bell Rattle	U.S.	c.1910-1920	$29
56	Plains Indian Rattle	U.S.	c.1950	$12
57	Pre-Columbian Rattle	U.S.	12th-14th century A.D.	$250
59	Navajo Rattles	U.S.	c.1960-1980	$40 and $50
64	Oil Painting	U.S.	c.1835-1840	$1,200
65	Oil Painting	U.S.	1824	$20,000
66	Oil Painting	U.S.	c.1830	$65,000
68	Miniature Painting	U.S.	c.1840	$750
69	Scrimshaw Teethers	U.S.	c.1850s	$500
70	Scrimshaw Teether	U.S.	c.1850s	$60
72	Scrimshaw Rattle	U.S.	mid-19th century	$500
73	Scrimshaw Rattle	U.S.	mid-19th century	$500
74	Tin Rattle	U.S.	c.1880-1890	$75
77	Painted Tin Rattle	U.S.	c.1910	$40
78	Tramp Art Rattle	U.S.	c.1860s	$225
79	Tramp Art Rattle	U.S.	mid-19th century	$175
80	Tramp Art Rattle	U.S.	c.1870	$400
81	Whimsy Rattle	U.S.	early 20th century	$100
82	Whimsy Rattle	U.S.	c.1890	$100
83	Whimsy Rattle	U.S.	early 20th century	$150
84	Cloth Rattle	U.S.	early 20th century	$5.00
85	Folk Art Rattle	U.S.	c.1930s	$3.00
86	French-style Rattle	U.S.	1870-1890	$200
87	Cat Rattle	U.S.	c.1910-1915	$150
88	Santa Claus Rattle	U.S.	c.1910	$200
89	Teething Ring Rattle	U.S.	c.1910-1920	$100
90	Watch Case Rattle	U.S.	early 20th century	$150
91	Tambourine Rattle	U.S.	1886	$500
92	Baby Head Rattle	U.S.	early 20th century	$150
93	Stub-type Rattles	U.S.	early 20th century	@ $400
94	Teether	U.S.	c.1910	$50
95	Teether	U.S.	c.1915-1920	$50
96	Teether	U.S.	c.1920-1930	$65
97	Art Nouveau Rattle	U.S.	c.1900	$175
99	Art Nouveau Rattle	U.S.	c.1900-1910	$400
101	Buster Brown Rattle	U.S.	c.1915	$125
102	Kewpie Doll Rattle	U.S.	c.1915-1920	$225
104	Art Deco Rattle	U.S.	1930	$65
105	Art Deco Rattle	U.S.	c.1930s	$65
106	Art Deco Tiffany Rattle	U.S.	c.1925	$350
107	Celluloid Rattle	U.S.	1930s	$75
108	Bowling Pin Rattle	U.S.	c.1935	$250
109	French Telephone Rattle	U.S.	c.1935	$100
110	Celluloid Rattle	U.S.	1930s	$10
111	Celluloid Rattle	U.S.	1930s	$20
112	Celluloid Rattle	U.S.	1930s	$20
113	Celluloid Rattle	U.S.	1930s	$35
114	Bakelite Rattle	U.S.	c.1940	$100

115	Humpty-Dumpty Rattle	U.S.	c.1940	$125
116	Spinner Rattle	U.S.	1950s	$60
117	Twist-handle Rattle	U.S.	1950s	$75
118	Conch Shell Rattle	U.S.	1950s	$100
119	Natural Wood Rattle	U.S.	1980s	$15
120	Bentwood Rattle	U.S.	1980s	$15
121	Artisan's Rattle	U.S.	1980s	$13
122	Artisan's Rattle	U.S.	1980s	$15
123	Good Humor Rattle	U.S.	1990s	$20
124	Miss Piggy Rattle	U.S.	1990s	$2.00
125	Snoopy Rattle	U.S.	1990s	$2.00
127	Oil Painting	England	1757	$7,500
128	Watercolor Painting	Scotland	c.1830	$3,000
129	Oil Painting	England	c.1835-1840	$4,500
130	Coral-and-bells Rattle	England	c.1720	$1,800
131	Coral-and-bells Rattle	England	c.1735	$1,500
132	Coral-and-bells Rattle	England	1807	$850
133	Coral and Vermeil Teether	England	c.1810	$700
134	Coral-and-bells Rattle	England	c.1745	$700
135	Coral-and-bells Rattle	England	1773	$825
136	Coral-and-bells Rattle	England	1793	$1,000
137	Coral-and-bells Rattle	England	1810	$9,000
138	Coral-and-bells Rattle	England	1861	$575
139	Coral-and-bells Rattle	England	1869	$650
140	Coral-and-bells Rattle	England	1880	$750
141	Owl Rattle	England	late 19th century	$175
142	Umbrella Rattle	England	1896	$150
143	Ivory Teether	England	late 19th century	$225
144	Ivory Teether	England	c.1900-1910	$300
145	Nursery Rhyme Rattle	England	c.1900	$85
146	Nursery Rhyme Rattle	England	c.1910	$125
147	Nursery Rhyme Rattle	England	c.1910	$125
148	Kate Greenway Teether	England	c.1900	$300
149	Jester Rattle	England	c.1900	$125
150	Jester Rattle	England	c.1900	$90
151	Jester Rattle	England	1909	$125
152	Sliding Monkey Rattle	England	c.1900	$800
153	Dormouse Rattle	England	c.1915	$100
154	Golliwog Rattle	England	1917	$200
155	Boy Scout Rattle	England	1912-1914	$350
156	Three Doll Rattles	England	1910-1915	$150-$300
157	Poupard Rattle	England	early 20th century	$850
158	London Bobby Rattle	England	c.1915-1920	$75
159	Scottish Leslie Rattle	England	c.1915-1920	$75
160	Dolly Rattle	England	c.1915-1920	$75
161	Dog's Head Teether	England	c.1920s	$400
162	Child's Head Rattle	England	c.1910-1920	$175
163	Thistle Rattle	England	c.1910-1920	$75
164	Acorn Rattle	England	1917	$75
165	Sheep Rattle	England	c.1920s	$40
166	Spaniel Rattle	England	c.1920s	$90
167	Folk Art Rattle	England	early 20th century	$60
168	Stuffed Cloth Rattle	Scotland	c.1940	$20
170	Empire Period Rattle	France	c.1803	$5,000
171	Empire Period Rattle	France	c.1800	$950

172	Punchinelle Rattle	France	c.1800	$750
173	Empire Period Rattle	France	early 19th century	$650
174	Pierced-work Rattle	France	1830-1850	$600
175	Embossed Rattle	France	c.1830-1850	$450
176	Prisoner's Work Rattle	France	early 19th century	$275
177	Angel Faces Rattle	France	mid-19th century	$450
178	Spinner Rattle	France	c.1840-1850	$450
179	Spinner Rattle	France	c.1840-1860	$350
180	Jester Rattle	France	1848	$275
181	Mandarin Rattle	France	mid-19th century	$500
182	Medieval Soldier Rattle	France	mid-19th century	$300
183	Two French Horn Rattles	France	1860-1870	$400 and $350
184	Mammiform Rattle	France	late 19th century	$175
185	Costume Plate Print	France	1887	$100
186	Marotte	France	early 20th century	$675
187	Set of Clown Rattles	France	c.1900	$250 set
188	Three Doll Rattles	France	c.1900	$60, $350, and $50
189	Postcard	France	1903	$5.00
190	Printed Tin Rattle	France	c.1903	$180
191	Painted Tin Rattle	France	1903-1904	$150
192	Beehive Rattle	France	1870-1890	$250
193	Beehive Rattle	France	early 20th century	$100
194	Angel Rattle	France	1915-1920	$100
195	Art Nouveau Rattle	France	c.1910	$75
196	Art Nouveau Rattle	France	c.1910-1915	$125
197	Art Nouveau Rattle	France	c.1910-1915	$450
198	Art Deco Rattle	France	c.1925	$250
199	Art Deco Rattle	France	c.mid-1920s	$75
200	Art Deco Rattle	France	c.1920s-1930s	$75
201	Costume Doll Rattle	France	1930s	$40
202	Costume Doll Rattle	France	1930s	$40
203	World War II Rattle	France	1940s	$50
204	Three Plastic Doll Rattles	France	1970s	$5.00 (for 3)
206	Mermaid Rattle	Italy	c.1700-1750	$1,200
207	Lion Rattle	Italy	c.1750-1800	$1,000
208	Hippocampus Rattle	Italy	mid-18th century	$1,500
209	Painted Tin Rattle	Italy	c.1914	$100
210	Spinner Rattle	Italy	c.1940s	$100
211	Spinner Rattle	Italy	c.1940s-1950s	$600
212	Pinwheel Rattle	Italy	c.1950s	$125
213	Horn-shaped Rattle	Spain	early 17th century	$2,000
214	Deer Rattle	Spain or Colony	17th century	$700
215	Openwork Rattle	Spain	early 18th century	$1,800
216	Clown Rattle	Spain	early 20th century	$75
217	Filigree Rattle	Spain	c.1950	$30
218	Pierced-work Rattle	Spain	20th century	$40
219	African Head Rattle	Spain	c.1950s	$25
222	Crystal-handle Rattle	Holland	early 18th century	$750
223	Crystal-and-bells Rattle	Holland	early 18th century	$750
224	Coral-and-bells Rattle	Holland	c.1750	$1,000
225	Regency-style Rattle	Holland	c.1830	$800
228	Vermeil Rattle	Holland	mid-19th century	$400
229	Pagoda Rattle	Holland	late 19th century	$350
230	Two Doll Rattles	Holland	c.1900-1910	$18 and $23
231	Art Nouveau Rattle	Belgium	early 20th century	$100

232	Art Deco Rattle	Belgium	c.1920s	$30
233	Peasant Girl Rattle	Germany	c.1900-1915	$65
235	Cottage Rattle	Germany	c.1900	$175
236	Coin Rattle	Austria	early 20th century	$800
238	Child's Ornament Set	Russia	c.1900-1915	$1,800
239	Woven Reed Rattle	Russia	c.1970s	$7.00
240	Woven Reed Rattle	Russia	c.1970s	$7.00
241	Gourd Rattle	China	1980s	$3.00
242	Lock Rattle	China	late 19th century	$150
243	Bell Rattle	China	early 20th century	$80
244	Bell Rattle	China	late 20th century	$20
245	China Export Rattle	China	mid-19th century	$250
246	China Export Rattle	China	c.1900-1910	$200
247	China Export Rattle	China	c.1900-1910	$175
248	China Export Rattle	China	early 20th century	$225
249	Drum Rattle	China	late 20th century	$3.00
250	Drum Rattle	Japan	c.1840	$60
252	Drum Rattle	Japan	c.1980s	$10
253	Woodblock Print	Japan	c.1880	$275
255	Art Deco-style Rattle	Japan	unknown	$35
256	Celluloid Rattle	Japan	c.1930s	$10
257	Santa Claus Rattle	Japan	1945-1955	$75
258	Tambourine Rattle	Japan	c.1970s	$20
259	Painted Clay Rattle	Japan	c.1970s	$20
260	Drum Rattle	Japan	c.1970s	$8.00
261	Doll Rattle	Japan	1985	$10
262	Hobby Horse Rattle	Japan	1970s	$6.00
263	Two Wood Rattles	Japan	1980s	@ $3.00
264	Archaic Rattle	India	2nd-1st century B.C.	$1,500
265	Mallet Rattle	India	early 20th century	$75
266	Ball Rattle	India	early 20th century	$75
267	Fringed Rattle	Nepal	early 20th century	$150
268	Two Small Teethers	India	c.1900	$350 and $40
269	Ball Rattle	India	early 20th century	$65
270	Dumbbell Rettle	India	c.1910	$225
271	Sea Horse Rattle	India	mid-20th century	$100
272	Foot Scraper Rattle	India	20th century	$350
273	Stuffed Doll Rattle	India	c.1970	$6.00
274	Sistrum Rattle	India	1997	$10
275	Pre-Columbian Rattle	Costa Rica	11th-13th century A.D.	$400
276	Pre-Columbian Rattle	Costa Rica	11th-13th century A.D.	$350
277	Pre-Columbian Rattle	Costa Rica	c.14th century A.D.	$350
278	Pre-Columbian Rattle	Mexico	10th-14th century A.D.	$300
279	Skull-Head Rattle	Mexico	1994	$2.00
280	Folk Art Rattle	Guatemala	1950s	$60
281	Basketry Rattle	Brazil	1895	$350
284	Gourd Rattle	Ivory Coast	early 20th century	$700
285	Twisted Straw Rattle	Kenya	1996	$4.00
286	Double-Drum Rattle	Zaire	early to mid-20th century	$450
287	Drum Rattle	Thailand	c.1970s	$1.00
288	Cowrie Shell Rattle	Philippines	early 20th century	$20
289	Folk Art Rattle	Indonesia	mid-20th century	$5.00
290	Butter Churn Rattle	Nepal	early 20th century	$350

Bibliography

Books on Toys and Paintings

Bell, Bernice. "Whistles with Coral and Bells," *Antiques Magazine*. December 1961.

Brant, Sandra and Elissa Cullman. *Small Folk: Childhood in America*. New York: E.P. Dutton. 1980.

Burton, Anthony. *Children's Pleasures*. Wappinger's Falls, New York: Antique Collector's Club. 1996.

Daikes, Leslie. *Children's Toys Throughout the Ages*. New York: Prager. 1962

Dribben, Jill. *Japanese Antique Dolls*. New York: Weatherhill. 1984.

Earle, Alice More. *Child Life in Colonial Days*. New York: McMillan. 1900.

Encyclopedia of World Art. New York: McGraw-Hill. 1962.

Farquar, Margaret C. *Indian Children of America*. New York: Holt, Reinhart and Winston. 1964.

Foley, Dan. *Toys Through the Ages*. Radnor, Pennsylvania: Chilton. 1962.

Groeber, Karl. *Children's Toys of Bygone Days*. London: Stokes & Company. 1928.

Haskell, Arnold and Min Lewis. *Infantantilia: The Archaeology of the Nursery*. London: Dennis Dobson. 1971.

Kritzen and Bachmann. *Illustrated History of Toys*. London: Abbey Library. 1961.

McClinton, Katherine Morrison. *Antiques of American Childhood*. New York: Clarkson. 1970.

McQuist, Dan and Debra. *Dolls and Toys of Native America*. San Francisco, California: Chronicle Books. 1995.

Marsella, Anthony. *Toys from Occupied Japan*. Atglen, Pennsylvania: Schiffer Publications. 1995.

Muensterberger, Dr. Werner. *Collecting: The Unruly Passion*. Princeton, New Jersey: Princeton University Press. 1993.

Schorsch, Anita. *Images of Childhood*. New York: Mayflower Press. 1979.

Spear, Jr., Nathaniel. *A Treasury of Archeological Bells*. New York: Hastings House. 1978.

Teruhies, Kitahara. *Japanese Tin Toys*. San Francisco, California: Chronicle Books. 1985.

Weiss, Harry M. *American Baby Rattles*. Privately printed. 1940.

White, Jan Manchip. *Everyday Life of North American Indians*. New York: Holmes-Miller. 1979.

Museum Publications:

Fowler Museum of Cultural History, University of California Publications. *Play and Ritual in African Sculpture*. 1996.

Heritage Plantation of Sandwich, Sandwich, Mass. *Is She or Isn't He? Identifying Gender in Folk Portraits of Children*. 1995.

Margaret Woodbury Strong Museum, Rochester, N.Y. *A Century of Childhood*. 1984.

Books on Hallmarks:

Bly, John. *Discovering Hallmarks on English Silver*. London: Aylesbury Press. 1981.

Bradbury, Frederick. *Book of Hallmarks*. London: Northend Publishing. 1972.

Bradbury, Frederick. *Marks of Origin on British and Irish Silverplate*. London: Northend Publishing. 1979.

Chaffer, William. *Handbook of Hallmarks on Gold and Silver*. London: William Reeves. 1969.

Green, Robert Alan. *Marks of American Silversmiths*. Self-published. 1984.

Grimwade, Arthur D. *London Goldsmiths and Their Marks*. London: Faber & Faber. 1978.

Jackson, Charles J. *English Goldsmiths and Their Marks*. New York: Dover Publications. 1921.

Kovel, Ralph M. *American Silvermarks*. New York: Crown Publications. 1989.

Wyler, Seymour B. *Book of Old Silver: American, English and European*. New York: Crown Publishers. 1937.

Other Information:

Catalogue of Collection: *L'Hochet a Travers Les Ages*, Ides Cammaert. BibliothecaWittockiana, Tervuren, Belgium.

Encyclopedia of Associations and Clubs
Gale Publishing Co.
835 Penobscot Building
Detroit, Michigan 48226-4094

Alberta, Eric and Art Maier. *Official Price Guide to Antiques and Collectibles*. New York: House of Collectibles. 1996. (This has a specific section on baby rattles.)